Making Numbers

Using manipulatives to teach arithmetic

Rose Griffiths

Jenni Back

Sue Gifford

OXFORD
UNIVERSITY PRESS

OXFORD
UNIVERSITY PRESS

Great Clarendon Street, Oxford, OX2 6DP, United Kingdom

Oxford University Press is a department of the University of Oxford.
It furthers the University's objective of excellence in research, scholarship,
and education by publishing worldwide. Oxford is a registered trade mark of
Oxford University Press in the UK and in certain other countries.

© Rose Griffiths, Sue Gifford, Jenni Back 2016

This edition published by Oxford University Press 2016

All rights reserved. No part of this publication may be reproduced, stored in a retrieval system, or transmitted, in any form or by any means, without the prior permission in writing of Oxford University Press, or as expressly permitted by law, by licence or under terms agreed with the appropriate reprographics rights organization. Enquiries concerning reproduction outside the scope of the above should be sent to the Rights Department, Oxford University Press, at the address above.

You must not circulate this work in any other form and you must impose this same condition on any acquirer.

Photocopying

The Publisher grants permission for the photocopying of those pages marked as 'can be copied' according to the following conditions. Individual purchasers may make copies for their own use or for use by classes that they teach. School purchasers may make copies for use by staff and students, but this permission does not extend to additional schools or branches. Under no circumstances may any part of this book be photocopied for resale

ISBN 9780198375616

3 5 7 9 10 8 6 4 2

Typeset by Aptara

Paper used in the production of this book is a natural, recyclable product made from wood grown in sustainable forests.

The manufacturing process conforms to the environmental regulations of the country of origin.

Printed in China by Leo Paper Products Ltd.

Oxford OWL

For teachers
Helping you with free eBooks, inspirational resources, advice and support

For parents
Helping your child's learning with free eBooks, essential tips and fun activities

www.oxfordowl.co.uk

MAKING NUMBERS
Using manipulatives to teach arithmetic

Contents

Chapter One: Introduction — 7

Chapter Two: Numbers to 12 — 13

Chapter Three: Exploring 9 to 20 — 35

Chapter Four: Exploring 15 to 50 — 57

Chapter Five: Exploring 25 to 200 and beyond — 79

Chapter Six: Looking forward — 106

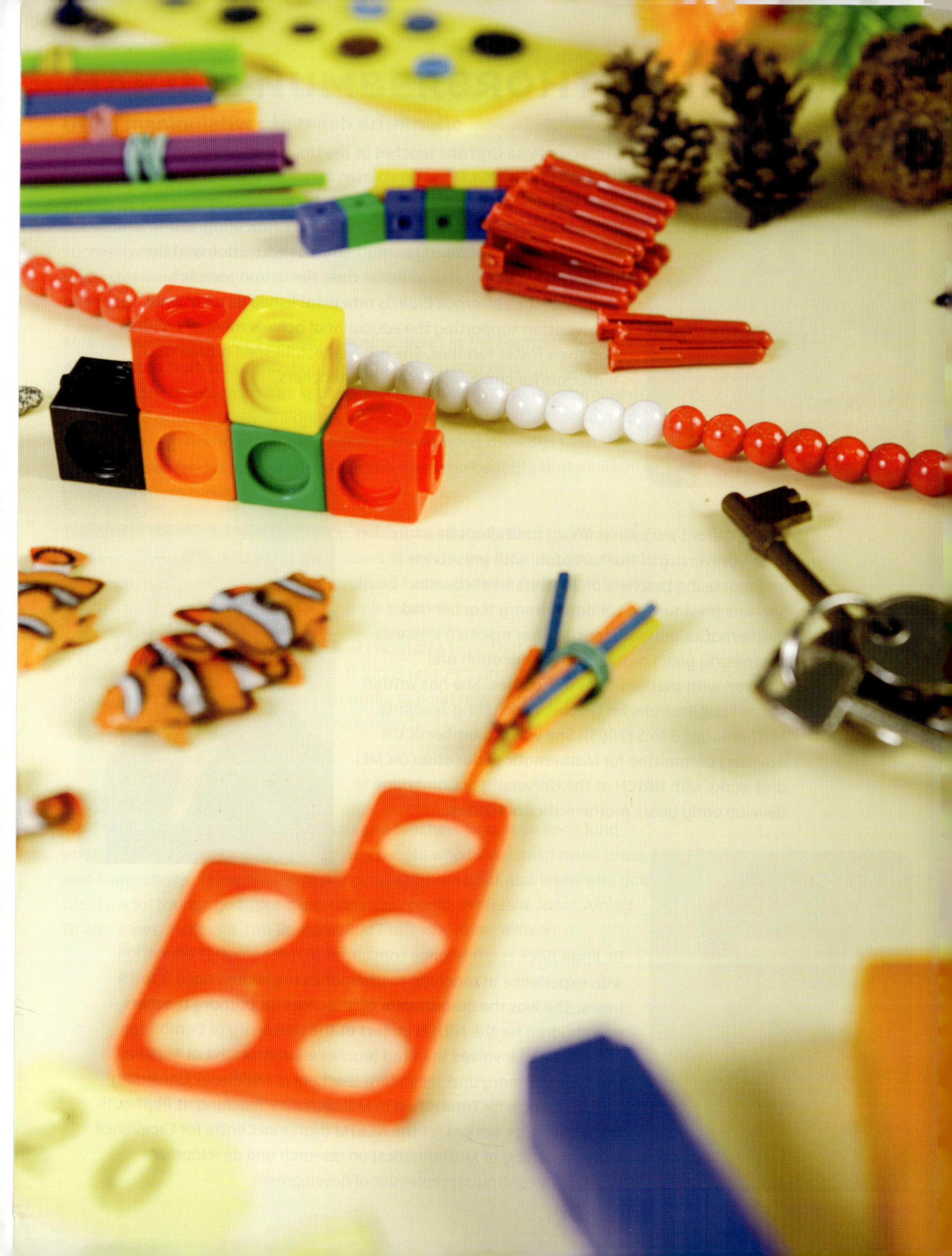

Chapter One: Introduction

We want mathematics to make sense to children.

Children need to develop 'number sense' to be able to draw on a range of strategies and knowledge about how numbers fit together. One way of helping them to understand and solve a problem is by providing practical resources to model the situation. Objects that can be used to develop learners' understanding of a mathematical situation and can be handled and moved by children are often called 'manipulatives'.

We can make numbers with all sorts of things. Some of them may be everyday objects, like toys, conkers, drinking straws or lolly sticks. Some equipment will be designed specifically for teaching arithmetic, such as wooden or plastic base ten equipment. Children or teachers may also make their own resources.

There are many ways of using manipulatives, and some approaches work better than others. Children will not benefit from just being taught to use manipulatives to follow a pencil and paper procedure. Instead we want a more effective and creative approach where children can focus on understanding mathematical ideas and solving problems. Rearranging objects helps children to try out new ideas. Children will choose from a range of strategies including using manipulatives, talking, drawing and writing, gradually moving towards a confident use of more abstract ways of working.

Manipulatives: items you can handle and move to learn more about counting and arithmetic.

Manipulatives work because they:
- help children make sense of arithmetic
- help teachers see what children understand
- increase children's engagement and enjoyment
- develop visual images and understanding
- help children to work together and share ideas
- are tools to help children: solve problems, investigate patterns and relationships, demonstrate results and reasoning
- provide a bridge to abstract thinking.

How does this work in practice? Let's take a look.

1 Introduction

How manipulatives help

In this example, Madhu was working with her class of 6 and 7 year-olds.

> If you just had 3s and 4s what numbers could you make?

> Let's start with numbers up to 12.

Madhu gave the children a range of equipment to use including interlocking cubes and strips of squared card.

---

1. Engagement and making sense of the problem

Jamie and Aisha (aged 7) started enthusiastically by making some 3s and 4s. They used these to make the doubles first: 3 + 3 and 4 + 4. Aisha then made 9 with three 3s, 12 with four 3s and then they got stuck.

The children were keen to use the manipulatives: they did not need to rely on reading and writing to make a start on the task. They felt confident to try things without fear of committing something to paper. The practical resources helped them to make sense of the problem: they had made 6, 8, 9 and 12.

---

2. Working and thinking together

Jamie said, "We've made all the ones you can. You can't make 10 and 11." But when Jamie and Aisha looked round at what other children in their class were doing, they saw that Leo had made 10. They realized they could use a combination of 3s and 4s together and so they started to find more.

Working in a pair builds confidence and provides immediate opportunities for discussion. Looking at what other children were doing challenged their thinking. They were able to use the 3s and 4s they had made to show their thinking to one another and support their reasoning.

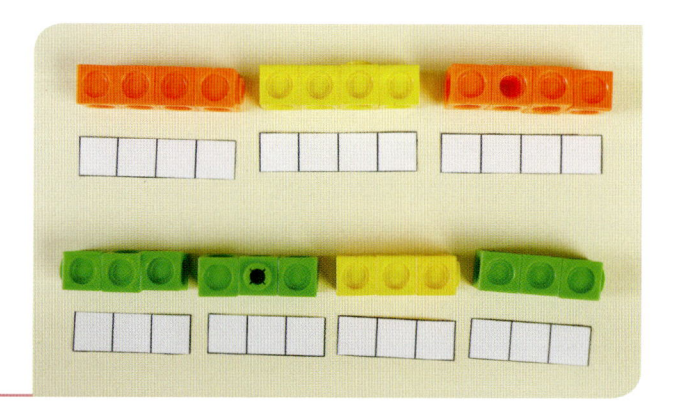

3. Representing and recording ideas

Madhu reminded the children to draw or write about what they had done.

Jamie's recording shows the numbers they used and the totals for each combination:

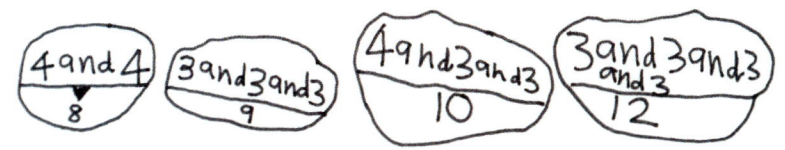

4 and 4 — 8 | 3 and 3 and 3 — 9 | 4 and 3 and 3 — 10 | 3 and 3 and 3 and 3 — 12

Recording helps children to develop mental images of what they have done. Madhu did not tell the children how to record their work. Jamie gained confidence through using the equipment and this supported him in devising his own systematic and meaningful method of symbolic recording. It showed his teacher that he really understood what he was doing. It will only take a nudge from her to help Jamie connect his personal number sentences with briefer, conventional equations.

Sometimes we need to help children become more observant and more careful in their drawing and writing. Other children produced different representations:

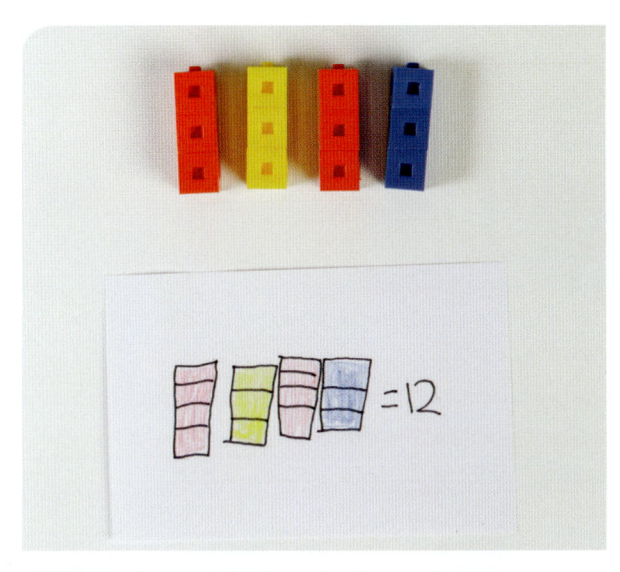

Did Hannah mean to show 4 + 3 + 4 + 3 or was it really four 3s? Madhu asked Hannah to explain her drawing to give her a chance to see the relationship.

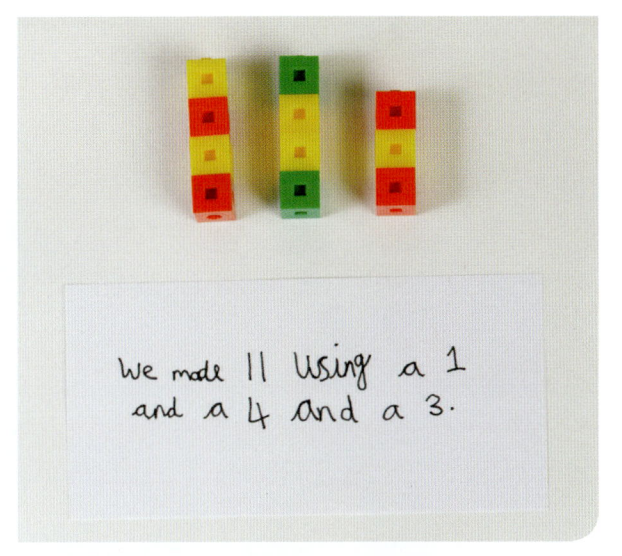

When Madhu asked, Daisy said they had used two 4s and a 3 to make 11. Madhu helped Daisy to correct her sentence.

1 Introduction

4. Sharing findings

The children and their teacher discussed the different ways they had used to make their numbers.

Children will often come up with questions while they look at other people's work. Teachers can offer prompts like those below if they do not arise naturally. These will help to challenge them and encourage them to explain their reasoning.

> You've done 4 add 3, we've done 3 add 4.
> Are they the same?
> I think they are because you can just swap them round.

> How did you make 11?
> Can we make it a different way?

> Did you make them all?
> Which ones can't we make?
> Can you explain why?
> Can we try with some bigger numbers?

Children can see they have approached the initial problem in different ways: some will have explored a range of varied examples whilst others will have found a pattern to follow. Similarly their written and drawn recordings will be very varied and all the children benefit from comparing them.

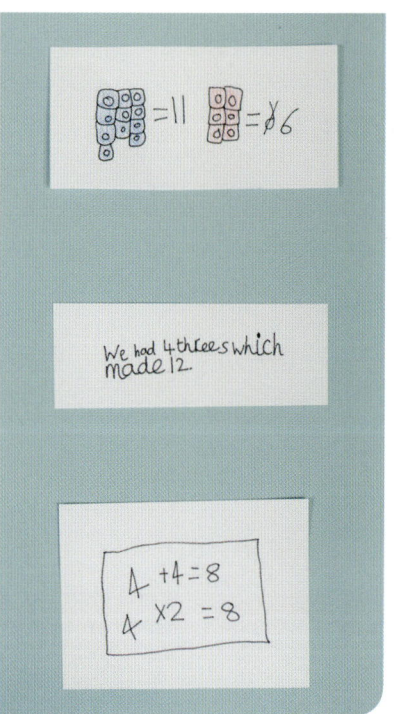

Number sense

In this book, we will look at activities and ideas that help children think about three key aspects of 'number sense', using a greater range of numbers in each successive chapter.

COUNTING

knowing the number names in order forwards and backwards

understanding how to count objects, events or actions in ones, and also in twos, fives, tens and so on

For example:

counting 16 beads, 5 claps, 8 stairs

count down as 5 buns are eaten

count up money in 10p pieces

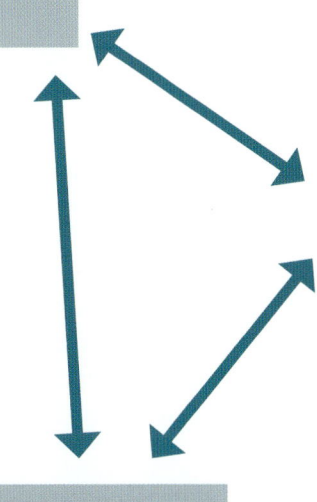

COMPARING

having a feel for the relative sizes of numbers

putting numbers in order

estimating

For example:

knowing that 6 is smaller than 8 but bigger than 2

being able to see that a group of objects has 'about 20' items

ordering 35, 3, 127, 53 from largest to smallest

COMPOSITION

understanding how each number can be made up in different ways by addition, subtraction, multiplication and division

knowing how our number system uses groups of hundreds, tens and ones

For example:

recognizing that 6 = 2 × 3 or 5 + 1 or 7 − 1 or can be made with a 4 and 2 rod

understanding that 125 can be made up from one 100, two 10s and five 1s or five 25s or in many other ways

1 Introduction

Classrooms for learning

There is no one right way of using manipulatives. This means that children need opportunities to explore, play, discover, discuss, spot patterns and analyze problems as part of the process of coming to understand and express their mathematical ideas.

None of us feels comfortable if we are asked to do something that is much too difficult for us. Similarly we may not want to waste our time practising something dull that we already know and can do. Open-ended tasks can provide us with the best opportunity to make sure that all children can engage with the mathematics – and they also help us assess each child's understanding.

A class of 9-year-old children was discussing whether 90 was divisible by six. Katie said it would not work, because 9 was an odd number and 6 was even. Some of her classmates agreed with her, but others began to argue. Olly said, "But 30 is in the 6 times table, so it must be OK."

Their teacher regularly encouraged the class to think of ways of explaining why something was true, so they started trying to convince Katie, using equipment and diagrams. She joined in the discussions, and ended up by saying, "I disagree with myself!" The classroom ethos made her feel comfortable enough to change her mind.

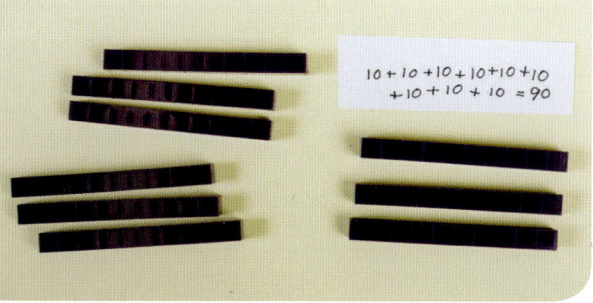

We want children to feel confident to try things out without worrying about being 'wrong'. This will only happen when children feel safe enough to say what they think. Manipulatives offer a vehicle for children to express what they are thinking, change their minds and develop their ideas.

Chapter Two: Numbers to 12

Counting is more difficult for children than you might think.

Some young children enjoy and are good at counting, others have had less experience. All will do best if we aim to provide a rich environment of situations and problems that the child will find engaging.
They need to see the purpose of counting, have the opportunity to change the situation, to experiment and to discuss what is happening with other people.

We need to find things that children want to count: why should they bother to be accurate, if the answer doesn't matter to them? Many everyday toys and other items can be used with a mathematical focus – not just bricks and counters. The stories that you can tell around many of the items suggested in this chapter will have benefits beyond just the mathematics – but they will also show that we can use numbers in everyday life in meaningful ways.

Children need repeated counting practice over a period of time, with frequent support from someone who can model the process. Adult 'coaching' is especially important in ironing out any glitches in the child's counting.

The largest number the child can count accurately will gradually increase, along with their confidence and fluency. Once a child can count, they can also start to consider the ways in which that number (and smaller ones) can be made from other numbers. For example, a child who can count to 7 accurately and reliably can also start to think about 2 add 3, or 6 take away one, or what comes after 4. They can decide which is bigger: 5 or 2? They can try to find different ways in which you can make 7. They will begin to gain a strong 'feel' for the size of a number.

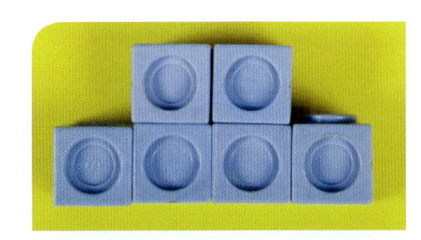

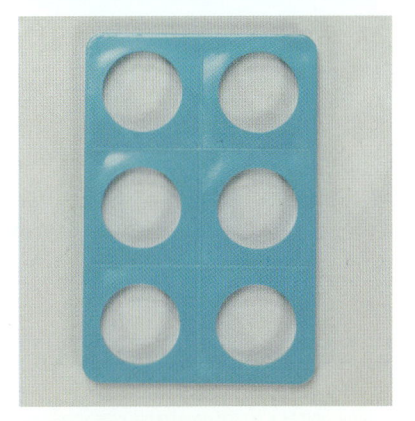

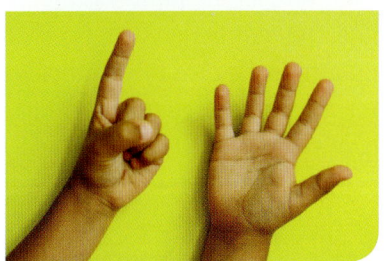

13

2 Numbers to 12

STARTING TO COUNT

Many mums, dads and carers count as they put children's arms in sleeves, fasten coat buttons or climb up or down stairs. Children become familiar with the counting sequence through these early experiences of listening.

Learning any new word takes time – you need to listen to someone else saying it, say it yourself, and gradually work out what it means. Young children have similar experiences with other new words.

Tibor, aged 1, was having his sleepsuit put on by his mum. She counted out loud as she did up the poppers, and she realized that although he could not say the words yet, his mouth was moving as she said, "One, two, three!"

"My 2-year-old son is just beginning to learn about colours. It's all a bit random at the moment – I say, "What colour are your wellies?" and he often shouts out "blue!" or "red!" even though they're yellow. He realizes I want a colour, but he doesn't know which word goes with which colour yet."

Even very small numbers can seem complicated. 'Two' can be your age, the number on your front door, the time you get to nursery … and there are also those other words that sound the same (too and to), to confuse you further! The child will begin to feel confident with *counting* to two when they have been able to see and hear other people counting two of many different things.

Many people think that counting is simply about saying the number names in the right order. However, there is a lot more to it than that, as many researchers have pointed out. We think it is useful to think about four key aspects:

NUMBER NAMES

There are many words to learn, they need to be in the right order and you need to be able to say the sequence forwards and backwards.

ONE NUMBER FOR EACH ITEM

Children need to match one number name to each item in turn, making sure that they do not count any twice or miss any out.

CARDINALITY

Children need to know that the last number in the count gives you the answer to the question "How many are there?" For example, although you might count, "1, 2, 3, 4" if there are four toy cars to count, if someone says, "How many are there?" you do not have to say, "1, 2, 3, 4"; the answer is just the last number: "4".

CONSERVATION

Children need to learn that the number of items in a group remains the same even if we rearrange them or count in a different order, so long as none have been added or taken away from the group.

The first three aspects have to be taught and can happen in any order – so, for example, a child might not know the number names yet, but they do know they must say one number for each item. Once all three aspects have been understood, the child's counting will become more accurate with bigger and bigger numbers. They will realize for themselves that the number in a group stays the same, that number is 'conserved', because they have counted small groups over and over again, and seen that they always get the same total.

Research link:

Gelman and Gallistel (1978) pointed out that children's counting involved understanding some key principles rather than just being based on rote learning of the number names. See also Buys (2001) and Munn (2008).

2 Numbers to 12

COUNTING MONKEYS

One of the first words that many young children learn is 'more'. It is a very useful word, especially when you combine it with pointing, because it can get you more food, more songs, or a story repeated over and over again. Children use the word in many inventive ways.

Omi was aged three, and he was interested in monkeys. When he visited his nan, he loved to search through her basket of soft toys, and found the monkey each time. She started to look out for monkeys in charity shops, and gradually added to the collection.

'When he found the first new monkey, he was thrilled, and counted both, touching each one: "Monkey, more monkey!" I counted them after him: "One monkey, two monkeys."'

The adult followed the child's interest and extended the opportunities for counting by finding more monkeys. She praised the child by nodding and smiling at his counting. She modelled the counting process herself.

'By the next visit, I had four monkeys in the basket. Omi lined them up on the floor to count them: "One monkey, two monkeys, more monkey, more more monkey!" I was impressed with his method of counting, and counted them out loud myself; "One, two, three, four monkeys." I wanted him to hear the numbers, and he copied me, starting with the last monkey: "One monkey, two, three, four monkeys."'

'A few weeks later, and by now I had five monkeys. Omi fished them out of the basket, throwing them on the floor as he found them: "One monkey, two monkeys, three, four, five. That's a lot of monkeys!" He had been practising counting at home, and he was confident with these number names. I was slightly disappointed. I think I was hoping for "more, more, more monkeys!"'

Several adults and other children were contributing to the child's learning of the number names, and showing him how to count. He was also watching children's television programmes that included counting, and singing counting songs at playgroup.

'Five monkeys were the most I could fit in my basket with the other animals. Omi still counted them when he came to visit, but now the counting seemed to be for a different purpose. He knew there were five, but he counted to make sure he had got them all.'

When there were just two monkeys, the child did not need to count them, to tell whether he had found them both. They were "big monkey" and "little monkey", and he recognized them. But with a larger number, counting is a convenient way of checking if you have them all.

Children's interests may be fleeting or persistent. We can follow their interests and introduce them to new ones. Their understanding of any aspect of mathematics will grow in fits and starts across a period of time, as they come across an idea in several different contexts and have the chance to explore it by themselves and with others.

2 Numbers to 12

TWO, THREE, FOUR, FIVE

Working with these smaller numbers is an important time for children to see how an adult counts, and to copy them. The materials you use should be a mixture of some that are identical, and others where they are different sizes, so children can gradually realize that the number of items is not reliant on the size of each one.

It is not unusual for younger children to be uncertain about what they are being asked to count – they need opportunities to 'sort out' the items they are interested in.

Ruby, aged 4, was not sure about counting these donkeys. Were the smaller ones donkeys, too? Or did they have a special name? She answered, "Two?" when asked how many donkeys there were. Ruby's teacher initially thought she could not count beyond two, then realized by Ruby's gestures and her puzzled face, that she might be uncertain about the animals.

The teacher said, "There are some baby donkeys, and some grown-up donkeys …" and Ruby counted again. She still didn't count accurately, because she counted one baby twice, so her teacher showed her how to move them out of the way as she counted them.

Work in a group

Vary your prompts and questions when you work with a group of children. Here are some examples:

> I've put three snails on my mat.
> Aaliyah, can you show us three fish?
> Dylan, three snakes?

> Let's check out each other's counting.

> How many shall we count now?
> Would you like to try four or five?

> Elijah, choose some spiders to go on your mat, and we'll say how many you have chosen!

> Swap with each other, so you can count a different animal.

> Swap *some* of your animals with each other.
> Charlie, you've got some spiders and some snails.
> How many spiders? How many snails? How many animals together?

Research link:

Wynn (1990) noted that counting out a specific number of items from a larger group is a useful assessment of children's ability to apply their counting skills.

Chapter Two: Numbers to 12

19

2 Numbers to 12

FIVE FRIENDS COUNTING

You can use five different toys in a story to explore counting to five and the combinations of numbers that make five.

The five animals shown here are the stars of a 3-minute animation called 'Five Friends Counting', available on *Oxford Owl*. You can use the animation as an introduction to a lesson, for children to watch at home and as a model for classroom activity that follows a similar pattern.

Watch the film straight through, then watch it again, pausing wherever you want children to answer a question or say what they notice.

Working with a 'cast' of five helps children to focus on many aspects of this number (and the numbers 0 to 4), including:

- counting forwards and backwards, and seeing what 'one more' or 'one less' makes
- recognizing the number words: none, one, two, three, four, five and the number symbols 0, 1, 2, 3, 4, 5
- combinations that make five: 0 and 5   1 and 4   2 and 3
  5 and 0   4 and 1   3 and 2
- 'missing numbers' within five (which is essentially subtraction: for example, 2 + __ = 5 can be solved by thinking about 5 - 2).

Using five different animals seems to help less confident children see that the five can be counted in any order, and in any combination, and there is still the same number. Perhaps it is easier to be reassured that the total stays the same when you can identify each animal individually.

Start by counting the animals onto the 'stage' and then off again . . .

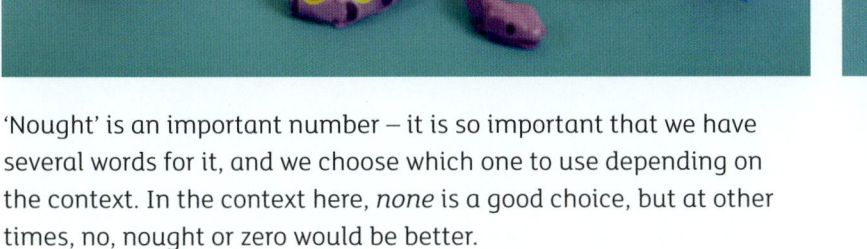

'Nought' is an important number – it is so important that we have several words for it, and we choose which one to use depending on the context. In the context here, *none* is a good choice, but at other times, no, nought or zero would be better.

Chapter Two: Numbers to 12

21

2 Numbers to 12

MAKING FIVE

Using props

Use props and activities to partition the group of five in different ways. Each scene can feature different numbers each time you re-enact it. Children can work with a partner, and act out, draw and write about different combinations of the friends for each activity.

3 friends sit on the boxes.

2 stay on the grass.

How many friends like carrots?

Chapter Two: Numbers to 12

1 friend is reading the paper

1 friend is reading the paper. 4 are not!

One is wide awake!

How many friends are sleepy?

2 friends are thirsty!

How many are thirsty? 3 friends are not.

23

2 Numbers to 12

Five friends wearing hats!

Make a hat for each of your animals from a circle of paper or felt:

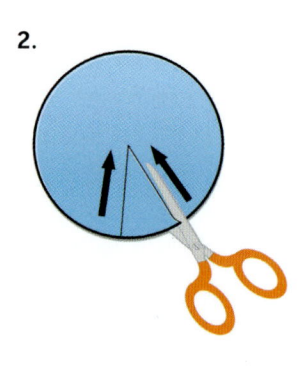

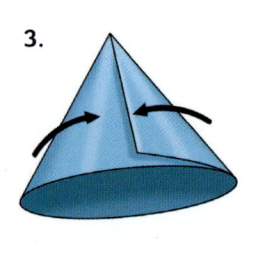

1.
2.
3.

When children have had a chance to experiment with several combinations that make five, demonstrate a systematic way of seeing them all, giving a hat to one more animal at a time:

Ask: "Five animals. How many have a hat on, and how many do not?"

Show these in order: 0 + 5, then 1 + 4, 2 + 3, 3 + 2, 4 + 1 and 5 + 0.

Five hats

This is an easy activity to act out with children too. Further practice in a random order will help children to learn the number facts that make five. You need five children with a hat each; when you say 'go', each child decides whether to put their hat on or not. You then ask the class: how many have a hat on, and how many do not? After a few turns, the combinations will be very familiar to many children.

24

Hidden numbers

Say: "Five friends go camping. How many are outside? How many are in the tent?"

How many in the tent?

This is a subtraction problem that many adults would solve quickly because they know the number fact 2 + 3 = 5. However, most young children will approach this problem in a different way. They may just guess, and see if their guess works, and then adjust it if needed. Or they may use their fingers to represent five animals: "There are two outside, so there must be three in the tent, to make five." It is also common to see a child pointing at animals that they are *imagining* in the tent – a strategy that shows they are beginning to find mental methods of solving a problem.

You can pose similar questions for children:

"Close your eyes and imagine five friends outside the tent. One friend goes into the tent. How many would be left outside now?"

Research link:

Hughes (1986) found that young children could solve addition and subtraction problems by imagining real objects, although they were not able to answer abstract questions. Using their fingers helped them bridge between abstract and concrete.

Chapter Two: Numbers to 12

2 Numbers to 12

COUNTING, DRAWING AND WRITING NUMBERS

The first numbers children learn to read will be ones that are important to them. Many children will start by recognizing 3, especially if they have cards and balloons on their birthday! As with letters, children need to see and use numbers in many forms, before they can start to write numbers for themselves. Many schools will have a handwriting policy that includes advice about writing numbers.

> Let's have this many cars! Have you put three cars in the car park?

> How many cars have you got? Can you find the number four to match?

> How many cars have you drawn? I've written the number on your drawing.

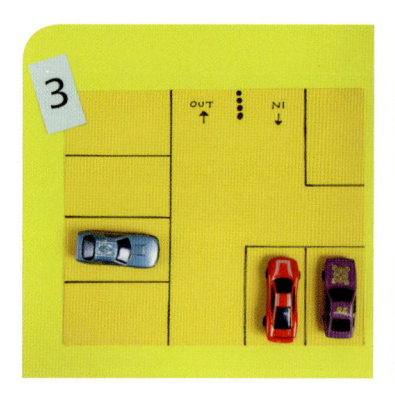

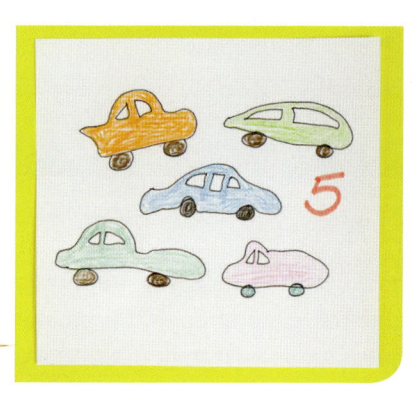

Young children's understanding of how we represent real things through models, photos and drawings can take some time to develop and using number symbols is a further step to abstraction. The move between 'concrete' and 'abstract' representations should not be rushed.

Research link:

Many researchers have examined the links between practical activity and symbolic representation. Bruner (1966) refers to enactive, iconic and symbolic modes of representation. Mason interprets these as three different worlds of experience: moving between manipulable objects; mental imagery or drawing; and abstract symbols (see Mason, Burton and Stacey 2010).

As adults, we often use written numbers alone to carry out a calculation problem – but when children are making a start on counting and arithmetic, it is important that they can spend time moving from concrete to abstract and back again, to really understand what is going on.

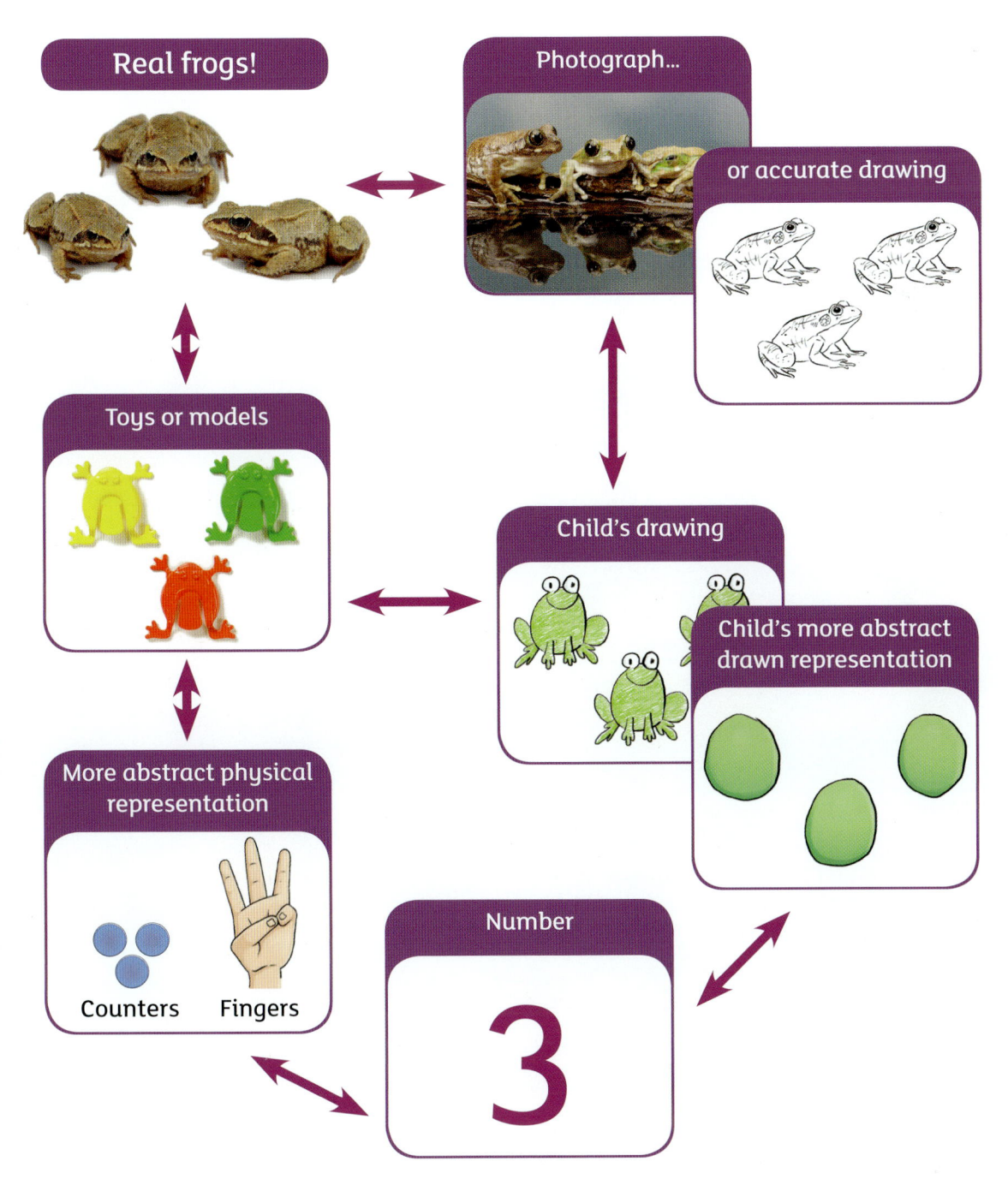

Chapter Two: Numbers to 12

Real frogs!

Photograph...

or accurate drawing

Toys or models

Child's drawing

Child's more abstract drawn representation

More abstract physical representation

Counters   Fingers

Number

3

2 Numbers to 12

FIVE, SIX, SEVEN, EIGHT

Counting and calculating are used in everyday life to solve problems or to keep track of what is happening. Providing a story or context for children's counting helps them to see a purpose in it, and to understand addition and subtraction from first principles.

Rabbit's blankets

Extend children's counting with different forms of suggestions and questions, and encourage them to make up stories of their own. Working with a partner will give them a chance to discuss what they are doing – and to rearrange, re-count, check and correct as they go along.

Make blankets from different colours of felt. How many blankets has Rabbit got on her bed?

> Let's give Rabbit three blankets. Can you give Rabbit four more blankets? How many blankets has she got now?

> Rabbit has six blankets. She says she is too warm, so let's take one off. How many has she got now?

> She says she is still too warm, so let's take another blanket off. How many has she got now?

> She says she is too cold, so let's put one back. How many has she got now?

> Baby Rabbit has three blankets on his bed. Daddy Rabbit has one blanket. Mummy Rabbit has two.
> Who has the most?
> Can you share the blankets out fairly?

Let children take turns in saying whether Rabbit is too warm or too cold, and change the number of blankets.

Use a different context for the same range of numbers, so that children can see their counting and calculating at work in a different situation.

Eight ducks in the lake

Eight is an interesting number – you can put it into 2s or 4s, organize it as an array and make it with several other combinations such as 5 and 3, or 1 and 7. An activity that concentrates on 8 items will help children see the many ways this number can be made.

Make a 'lake' from a sheet of blue card, add a 'nest' from green tissue paper and a 'deck' of wood, and your ducks have three places to be, encouraging children to make up stories of 8 using three numbers, not just two. As well as using the practical equipment, children can draw or paint scenes of their own and write the number of ducks in each place.

There were 2 ducks in the nest, 3 ducks in the water and 3 ducks on the deck. How many altogether?

Children can take turns with a partner to throw the dice and then move that many ducks around. The partner has to say how many are in each place!

Chapter Two: Numbers to 12

2 Numbers to 12

NUMBERS IN AND OUT OF PATTERNS

Some arrangements of numbers are very familiar in our everyday life, and it soon becomes possible for children to 'see' how many there are, without having to count. This is called subitizing. The patterns on a dotty dice or on dominoes are obvious to an adult, but do remember to let children count for themselves at first, to check. The pattern of 6 seen on a dotty dice is similar to that in an egg box – two rows of 3. This recognizable pattern can make it easier for a child to see combinations of numbers that will make that total. For example, 6 can be made with 3 + 3, or 2 + 2 + 2, or 4 + 2.

Children also need to think about each number more randomly:

How many tops are spinning?
How many are still?

Children can use items of equal size to make their own patterns, to make themselves more familiar with particular numbers. Drawing their pattern afterwards will help them think more carefully about the pattern they have made.

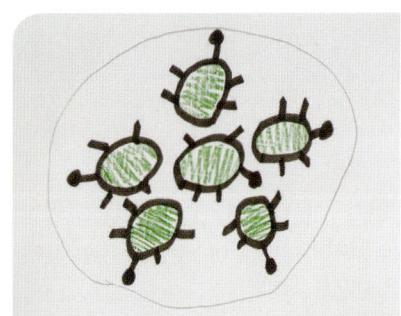

WHO HAS MOST?

Comparing two numbers when one is very small and the other is much larger is easy.

It is much harder to tell when the numbers are closer and counting is the best way of checking.

'Who has the most?' is an activity that helps children think about the relative size of numbers. Choose two toy animals; sit them opposite each other, with a dish each. Use pennies or counters and a dice to play. A pair of children can play together, to talk about what happens.

How to play

- Throw the dice for one animal, and give them that many counters in their dish.
- Throw the dice for the other animal. Give them that many counters.
- Decide: which animal has most? Count their counters to check.

Now throw the dice again for each animal, to give each animal more counters.

- Decide now: which animal has most? Count to check.

Vary the game by changing the dice: first use a dotty dice, then try a 1 to 6 numbered dice, then a 0 to 5 numbered dice, then a dice with bigger numbers. Or change the number of animals: first 2 animals, then 3, then 4, to see who has the most each time.

2 Numbers to 12

NINE, TEN, ELEVEN, TWELVE

As children extend the range of numbers they are working with, they will begin to find ways of making their counting and calculating more efficient. Sometimes they will discover these strategies on their own, but often they will learn them from other people.

Children's adding usually follows these stages: for example, when adding 2 and 4:

At first, the child will 'count all': "1, 2 buttons here; 1, 2, 3, 4 buttons here; 1, 2, 3, 4, 5, **6** buttons altogether."

Then they begin to 'count on' from the first group: "1, 2 buttons here; 1, 2, 3, 4 buttons here; so 3, 4, 5, **6** buttons altogether."

Lastly, they may realize that because they can add in any order and still get the same answer, they could save time by 'counting on from the larger number': "1, 2 buttons here; 1, 2, 3, 4 buttons here; so 5, **6** buttons altogether."

Encourage children to make up simple addition and subtraction stories, using a variety of contexts and equipment. Acting out these word problems with representative equipment helps children think about which ones involve adding and which are taking away.

> There were 7 red dinosaurs. Then 4 blue dinosaurs came along. How many were there altogether?

> There were 11 ants, but 11 of them were eaten by an anteater! How many were left?

Making number sentences

The key element to children developing confidence about using a written format for a number problem is that they solve it with equipment first. They can then experiment with drawing, writing and using a calculator, as well as trying to imagine the problem, and working out an answer with their fingers or in their head. Using more than one approach to the same problem helps you understand the 'story' better and allows you to check your answer.

Using a calculator alongside counting equipment gives children a reason for learning not just the number symbols but also the addition and equals symbols.

- Jassa counted up 7 red and 4 blue dinosaurs, and knew the total was 11.
- His teacher explained that the calculator could add numbers up, and showed him the + key, and then = .
- Jassa pressed the keys on the calculator to check his counting, and read the display:

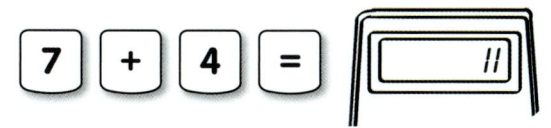

$7 + 4 = 11$

Jassa could see from this how to make a number sentence to match the 'dinosaur story'. It helped him make the transition from practical activity to a more formal written record.

You can use a similar approach with subtraction problems.

Nicki and Logan were working together. Nicki made up this story:

- "There were 12 turtles in the lake, then 5 swam away. How many were left?"
- Logan counted 12 turtles, made 5 swim away, and answered: "Seven."
- Nicki pressed the keys on her calculator to check:

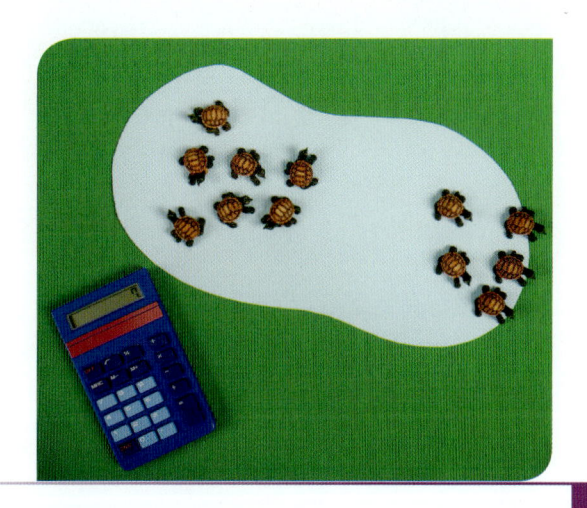

$12 - 5 = 7$

Chapter Two: Numbers to 12

33

2 Numbers to 12

NOT TOO FAR, NOT TOO FAST

When children are working with numbers to 12, our priorities are to help them become more expert at:

- counting accurately
- comparing numbers of different sizes
- seeing as many ways as possible of making any given number from other numbers
- solving and creating number problems and stories.

When children engage in purposeful practical activity, they become confident and fluent with counting and calculating. They will also develop familiarity with a growing repertoire of number facts. Practical activity coupled with thinking, describing, discussing, drawing and modelling will build children's understanding and number sense.

Five friends each invite a friend to their party.
How many hats and plates will we need?

Chapter Three: Exploring 9 to 20

Understanding the numbers to 20 depends on children's knowledge of the numbers to 10.

When working with numbers over 10, children frequently need to use bonds for smaller numbers. For instance, with 17 − 4, a child can use the fact 3 + 4 = 7 to find the answer, 13. We therefore begin with a focus on numbers to ten in different representations, to consolidate children's knowledge of all the numbers up to ten in more systematic ways.

This chapter focuses on the different ways numbers to 20 can be taken apart and put back together again, linking addition and subtraction. As discussed in Chapter Two, children will need lots of practice in counting, including learning the new number names from 11 to 20. With more things to count there are more chances of losing track, so emphasising one-to-one counting continues to be important.

Part of understanding numbers 11 to 19 involves seeing how they are made of ten and some ones. It helps if children have a very strong sense of the ten-ness of ten and how the numbers in order are 'one more than' and 'one less than' their neighbours, as in a 'staircase' pattern.

Exploring and having the opportunity to play freely is an important stage in working with any practical equipment. Manipulatives can help children to notice patterns and to create their own, for example spotting groups of 5 and 10, or odd and even numbers. Different representations emphasize different aspects, so we prompt children to "Say what you see" and to consider, "What's the same and what's different?"

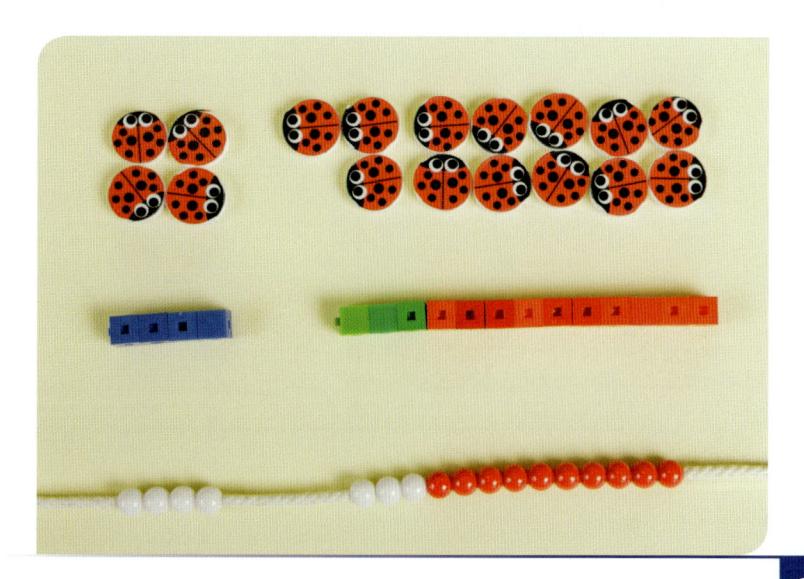

3 Exploring 9 to 20

USING FIVES

By using their fingers, children learn that 5 and 5 make 10 and they soon recognize the dice pattern for 5. Several structured manipulatives use patterns of 5.

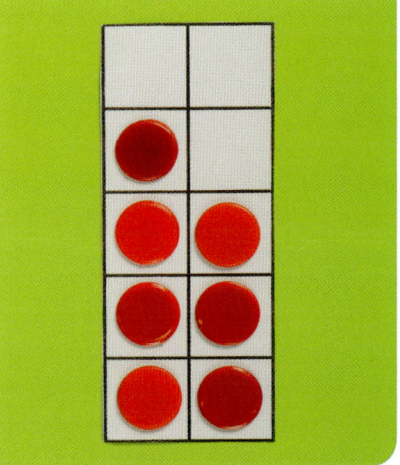

The pattern of two 5s enables children to see numbers like 7 as '5 and 2', while also showing 7 as 3 less than 10.

Hungarian number pictures

Every child in Hungarian primary schools has these 10 boards with the familiar dice pattern of 5, which they use with double sided counters to explore numbers to 10 and then numbers to 20.

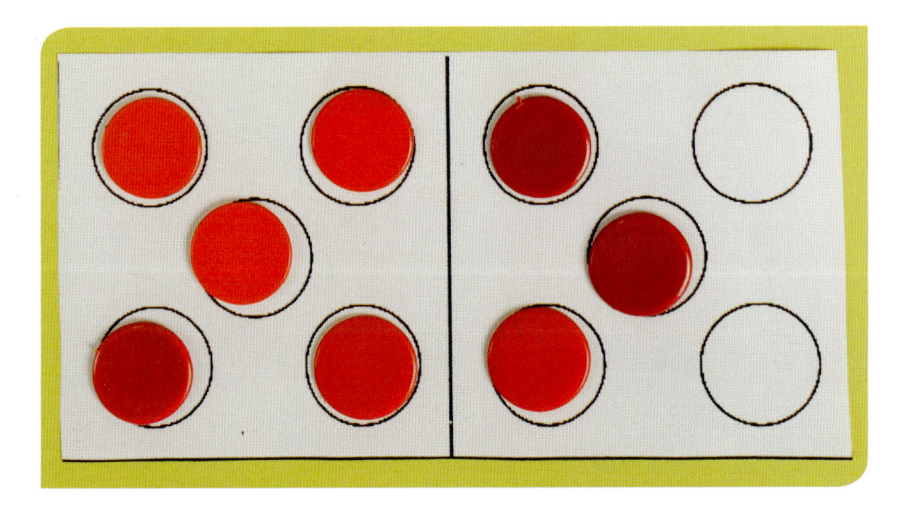

Making 7

Turning the counters over one at a time helps children to see that the number of counters remains the same. They can also spot the pattern of the number of red counters going up, as the number of yellow counters goes down.

Each group of three numbers gives us a linked set of number facts.

| 7 | 5 | 2 |

Children can suggest number sentences:

7 is 5 and 2
7 take away 2 is 5

Later, after lots of experience, children can match written number sentences with the images they make.

7 = 5 + 2   7 − 2 = 5   2 + 5 = 7
7 − 5 = 2   2 + 5 = 5 + 2

It is important that children understand that the equals sign means 'is the same as'. They need to realize that both sides of the equation must 'balance' and that a total can come first.

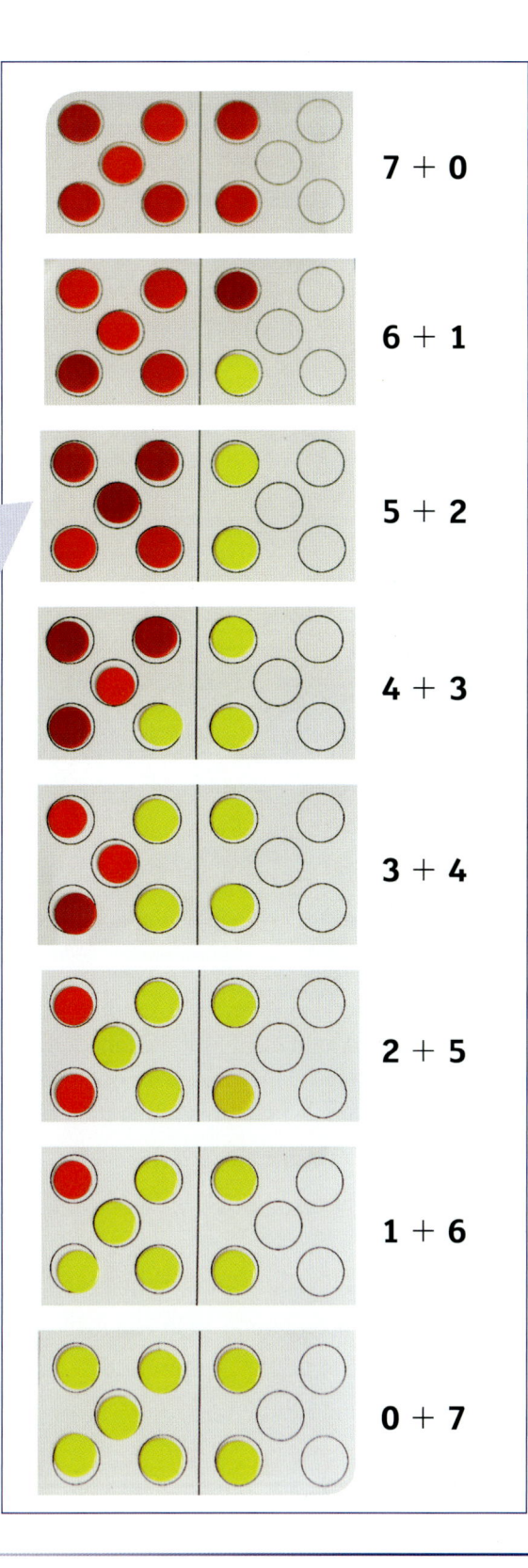

7 + 0
6 + 1
5 + 2
4 + 3
3 + 4
2 + 5
1 + 6
0 + 7

Chapter Three: Exploring 9 to 20

37

3 Exploring 9 to 20

TEN FISHES IN THE SEA

Children will probably use number bonds for 10 more than any others. You can use 10 toys to explore this important number.

The shoal of paper fish shown here are from a 3-minute animation called 'Ten Fishes in the Sea', available on *Oxford Owl*. You can use the animation as an introduction to a lesson, for children to watch at home and as a model for classroom activity that follows a similar pattern using your own fish.

The animation shows fish swimming about quite quickly, which presents the hardest kind of counting challenge – moving images on a screen! Counting will be easier with objects children can handle themselves, so we suggest children make their own 'fish' or choose other small toys.

The 10 fish are used to explore the different ways 10 can be made. Key ideas include:

- counting forwards and backwards in ones and twos
- partitioning and recombining 10 in equal and unequal groups
- number bonds for 10 and the commutativity of addition
- linking addition and subtraction
- using number sentences
- recognizing patterns with 2, 3 and 5.

Counting things and spotting patterns

It is important for children to be able to count backwards as well as forwards so that they know the number sequence inside out.

Children can also count in twos, which familiarizes them with the even numbers: 2, 4, 6, 8, 10.

When adding or subtracting one or two objects at a time, children can look for a pattern. You can ask children to predict how many there will be next. Starting with 9 and taking away pairs produces the decreasing pattern of odd numbers: 9, 7, 5, 3, 1.

> What do you think will come next? How do you know?

> What do you notice about the numbers?

> Is there a pattern? What can you say about the pattern?

Counting in twos can be tricky: a valuable activity is to invite children to count a set of objects, firstly in ones and then in twos. They should get the same number both times!

Children can also explore odd and even numbers to see which numbers are made of pairs or can be split into two equal groups.

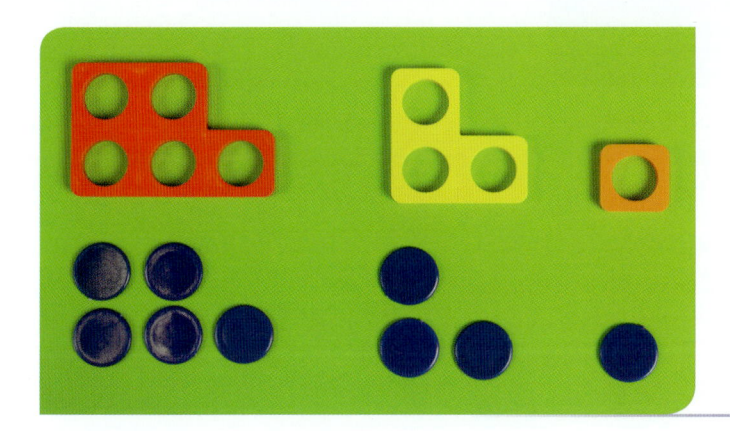

Research link:

Mulligan and Michelmore (2009) found that children who could recognize patterns and structures in images were better at maths. They suggested that children need to be taught to look for patterns and explore similarities and differences between them. Children therefore need to *say what they see*, make patterns for themselves, copy others, including from memory, and predict how they will continue.

Chapter Three: Exploring 9 to 20

3 Exploring 9 to 20

MAKING TEN

Ten can be made in lots of different ways.

How has this 10 been made?

It's 1 and 2 and 3 and 4.

Children can explore different ways of making 10. This creates discussion about the important idea of numbers being made up of other numbers, and seeing a number as part of another – 'part-whole' relationships.

Say what you see: what numbers can you see hidden inside this number?

I knew it was 10 because I saw 5 and 5.

You can then ask them to compare their patterns by asking, "What's the same and what's different?" This kind of exploration is valuable for all numbers both bigger and smaller than ten.

Research link:

Nunes & Bryant (2009) emphasize the importance of children seeing any number as composed of other numbers e.g. 5 as comprising 3 and 2. This is sometimes referred to as part-whole understanding, which many researchers see as essential to addition and subtraction.

Adding in any order

Experimenting with adding numbers in a different order will help to convince children that you can add numbers in any order and still get the same total. This is called the commutative principle of addition.

In the 'Ten Fishes in the Sea' animation the number bonds to 10 are shown in patterns like these:

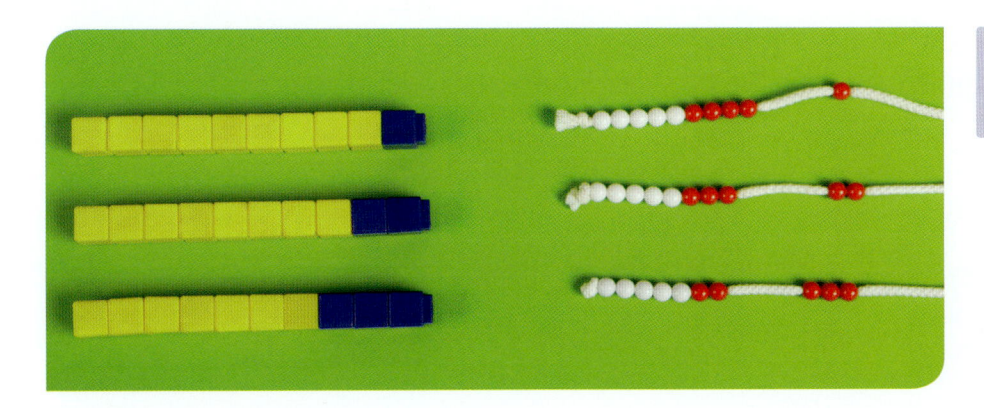

What do you notice? What comes next?

This also demonstrates the useful addition strategy of *compensation*: if you add to one number and take the same number off the other it does not affect the total. The Hungarian number pictures also showed this by turning over counters one by one.

3 Exploring 9 to 20

PARTITIONING

A number of objects can be split into more than two groups: this helps develop children's confidence in handling numbers. Investigating different ways of making equal groups from a number introduces ideas of multiplication and division.

We can swim in twos

We can swim in fives

Ten can be divided into 5s or 2s.

Children will also enjoy exploring combinations of equal and unequal groups.

I made 3 and 3 and 3 and there is 1 at the end.

I made two groups of 4 and a 2.

Making patterns for a chosen number helps to develop children's flexibility in thinking about numbers, gaining familiarity with the ways they are made, which they can then apply to bigger numbers.

Research link:

Gray and Tall (1994) found that children who were more effective mathematical thinkers were able to use a few number facts flexibly, to suit the problem. Children who used fixed procedures involving counting tended not to do this, which made calculations more laborious. Boaler (2009: 139) emphasizes that 'high achieving students … engage in flexible thinking when they work with numbers, decomposing and recomposing numbers'.

Hidden numbers

This game can be played with 10 objects, hiding different numbers in a pot, under a cloth or behind a screen, and asking children how many are hidden. Children might use their fingers to work out the answer or imagine the hidden items and count them. With practice children will become confident with more number facts for 10 and be able to just give an answer.

Can children work out how many dinosaurs are hiding?

Children in pairs can hide numbers for each other, using different scenarios, such as dinosaurs hiding in caves or monkeys hiding bananas under a leaf. Children's own recording of what they have found out will provide teachers with further insights into their thinking.

This game can then be played with bigger and smaller numbers.

10 and 10 make 20

Once children are confident with numbers up to 10, they can use what they know to develop their understanding of numbers to 20.

3 Exploring 9 to 20

THE TRICKY TEENS

The words for numbers over ten are notoriously tricky in English. In some Asian languages and in Welsh, numbers follow a verbal pattern of "ten, ten-one, ten-two, ten-three", so that their meaning is transparent. In English children must learn all the counting words to twenty individually with little obvious pattern: eleven, twelve, thirteen, and so on. It all becomes easier after twenty!

As with smaller numbers, counting objects is an important way of becoming familiar with this range of numbers – for example, gaining a 'feel' for how big 15 is.

Counting collections

Children like to count collections of small objects such as jewels, conkers, shells, small toys, plastic spiders – anything where they are interested in finding out how many there are. Working with a partner gives children the chance to talk about their counting and check each other's work.

They need to work in two ways:

Children take it in turns to put some items on the table and ask their partner, "How many are there?"

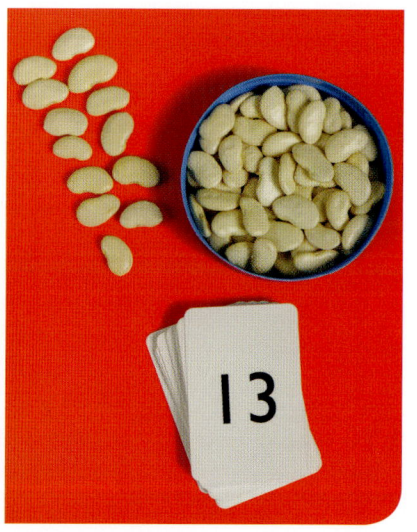

Take it in turns to choose a card from a set of 0 to 20 cards and count out that many.

Estimating

Once children become more confident with the size of teen numbers, you can challenge them to estimate before they count:

> How many do you think there could be?

> How many do you think you can pick up in a handful / scoop / spoonful?

> Did you pick up more or less than you thought?

Comparing and ordering

Children can compare several collections and put them in order of size, either from bigger to smaller or from smaller to bigger.

Research link:

We should not underestimate the time young children take to understand numbers to 20. According to Sarama & Clements (2009), children often miss out 13 and 15 when learning to count, possibly due to the challenging pronunciation or to the lack of a consistent pattern. Fuson (1988) pointed out that 'English-speaking children have a much more difficult task in learning the sequence of numbers'.

Chapter Three: Exploring 9 to 20

45

3 Exploring 9 to 20

TEN AND SOME ONES

A key aspect of the numbers 11 to 19 is that they include a group of 10. This is a surprisingly difficult idea for some children and they need plenty of practice with splitting collections of objects into 10 and another number.

Place value cards are particularly useful to show numbers made up of '10 and ...'.

Children in pairs can count a group of objects, partition it into 10 and some ones, and then match to place value cards. They can also add the partitioned numbers on a calculator, to see that 10 + 6 = 16 and 6 + 10 = 16.

Structured resources such as bead strings or the rekenrek give children the experience of grouping objects into 'a 10', with clues in the colour groups of 5s. As with Hungarian number pictures, the '10 and some ones' structure is shown with two 5s making 10. Many people find it easier to see 'the 10' with two groups of five, rather than with, for instance, a stick of 10 identical cubes.

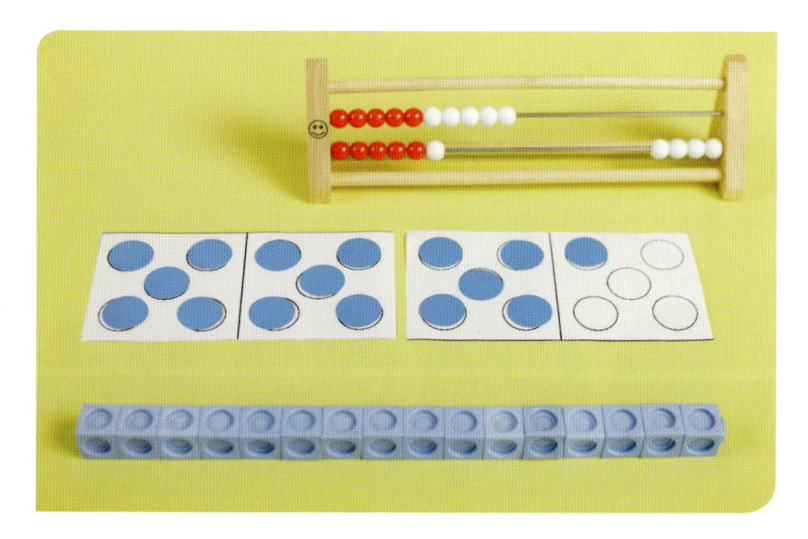

Reading and writing the teen numbers

Before writing the teen numbers children need to become familiar with reading them. Children can:

- count up and down a number line to 20
- order a set of 0 to 20 number cards
- count a group of objects and find the matching number card or
- read a number card and count out that many objects.

The mismatch in the way the teen numbers are written and spoken can mislead children into writing 'fourteen' as '41', because they start by saying 'four'. Some teachers playfully count 'tenty-one, tenty–two...' up to twoty, and then twoty-one, twoty two...! This is just a short-lived joke to make a point: however, addressing potential confusions explicitly can help children to understand the numbers.

Here are three ways of helping children to check how to write a teen number. In this example we use '14'.

14 is 10 and 4.

Use place value cards to make your number.

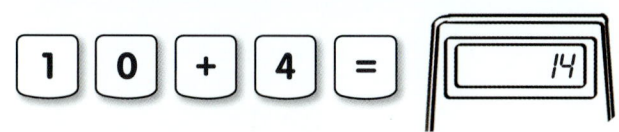

Make your number on a calculator.

Look at a number line or a ruler.

Chapter Three: Exploring 9 to 20

47

3 Exploring 9 to 20

BEAD STRINGS

Bead strings use patterns of 5 or 10 in alternating colours to provide a convenient structure for counting. Initially children need opportunities to move the beads and say what they see. Using a string of 20 beads gives children a clear sense of the size of twenty and how it is made up.

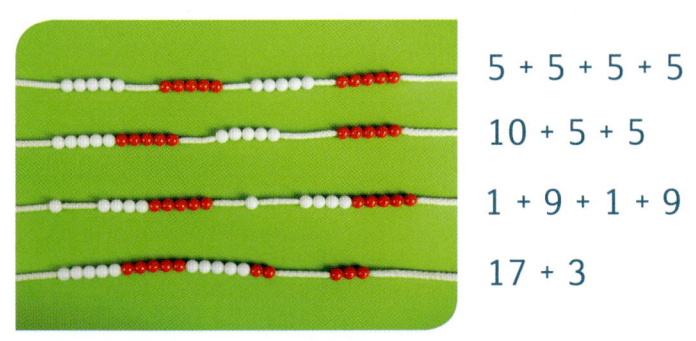

5 + 5 + 5 + 5

10 + 5 + 5

1 + 9 + 1 + 9

17 + 3

How many ways can you show 20 on your bead string?

Shut your eyes and tell me how to make…

Children can take turns to choose a number between 10 and 20 and challenge each other to describe it and then show it on a bead string.

How can you make 17?

I can do 5 add 5 add 5 add 2

Turn your bead string round!

Bead strings are good for showing the commutativity of addition. For example, ask children to show 15 add 3, then turn the string round and say what they notice: 3 add 15.

Complements to 20

Pairs of children can take turns to choose a number and challenge their partner to say and show how many more to make 20. This encourages children to use the number bonds for 10 to find bonds for 20. Children can record the complements they find in their own way.

After putting the bead strings away, ask the children to visualize the bead string to answer similar questions.

We have six. How many more to make 20?

6

48

Number lines and bead strings

Manipulatives can help children to understand the principles that lie behind the symbols and diagrams we use to represent aspects of number. Number lines are an example of an abstract representation that children may find puzzling.

One way of helping children to understand number lines is to link them to countable objects, such as bead strings. They can make their own number line to match a bead string.

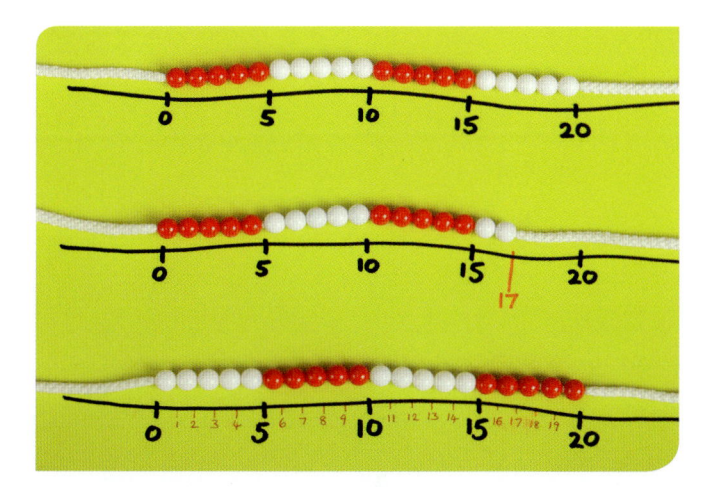

An alternative transition to the number line is to use a ruler alongside centimetre cubes or coloured rods.

Number tracks are useful for whole number counting.

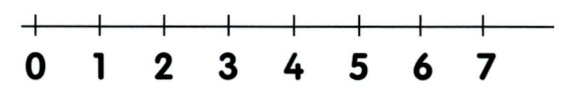

Number lines are useful for whole number counting and, later on, for fractions, decimals and negative numbers.

Research link:

Sarama and Clements (2009:119) concluded that *'there is much to be cautious about in considering the use of the number line as a representation for beginning arithmetic'*. In the Netherlands, they found that teaching children to find a number on a bead string and then on a number line helped children to develop mental calculation (Beishuizen, 2010).

3 Exploring 9 to 20

STAIRCASE

Children are fascinated by 'staircase patterns', which show the important idea that each whole number is one more and one less than its 'neighbours'. These staircases offer lots of opportunities for children to get involved in ordering and examining the teen numbers: children enjoy creating and sorting mixed up staircases and talking about what they notice.

Making the 11 to 20 staircase helps children to see these numbers as made up of ten and another number. Children can:

- **Continue a staircase from 10 to 20**

  What number comes next? How do you know?

  Because it's like ten, 1,2,3,4.

- **Sort out a mixed up staircase**

  How did you know where that one went?

- **Secretly hide one and close the gap**

  Which one is missing?

  How do you know?

  > 14 because there's a bigger step there.

- **Find a written number to match a stick**

  That's 17 – easy peasy – because there's 7 and then there's ten.

- **Find a stick to match a written number**

  How did you know that stick was 18?

  Fawkia started by pointing at 20:

  I knew one less would be 19 and one less would be 18.

Coloured rods

Coloured rods are very powerful, because they encourage children to think about relations between whole numbers and use their number facts. However, children first need time to understand how the rods represent numbers and to play with them, perhaps making a staircase to help.

Children can experiment with staircases for numbers over ten. For example, adding 2s to the 1 to 10 staircase results in the 3 to 12 staircase.

> Here's a 5 and a 7. Which rod fits in the gap?

> Can you find other pairs that have a difference of 2?

Chapter Three: Exploring 9 to 20

3   Exploring 9 to 20

MAKING 19

Caroline was working with her class of 7-year-olds. First they revised the addition and subtraction facts for 9 by making a number rod 'wall' for 9.

They used this to help complete missing number sentences like 4 + ? = 9. Caroline then invited the children to construct the bond patterns for 19. Alex pointed at the orange 10 rods and said, "You just need to add ten on to each one."

Caroline then wrote missing number sentences for 19 and asked the children to explain their solutions to each other, using the rods.

4 + ? = 19   19 − ? = 4   19 − 4 = ?

Familiarity with the rods enabled the children to spot the pattern linking the bonds for 9 with the bonds for 19. The children then explored similar patterns for the numbers from 15 to 20.

Chapter Three: Exploring 9 to 20

A number rod wall can help children to see the link between the bonds for 9 and the bonds for 19.

3 Exploring 9 to 20

DOUBLES AND NEAR DOUBLES

Doubling – adding a number to itself or multiplying it by two – is something that children find interesting. Using the same number of fingers on each hand, children can quickly learn that 1 add 1 makes 2 or double 5 is 10.

It is interesting to show doubles in different ways: try single items, drawn 10 frames and the rekenrek (a Dutch 'reckoning rack'). Doing plenty of doubling numbers 0 to 10 gives children a repertoire of key number facts from which to derive other facts. The idea that double 0 is 0 is very important and easy to understand if you do it with practical equipment along with other facts. Double nothing is nothing!

Near doubles

The doubles facts are very useful as children can use them to derive other facts as 'near doubles', e.g. 6 + 6 = 12, so 6 + 7 = 13. Another way to think about near doubles is to take 1 off one number and give it to the other, so 4 + 4 = 5 + 3.

If you know this, what else do you know?

Ask children to start with a doubles fact that they know and show you what else they know or can work out. Encourage children to be as creative as they wish by asking: "What else could you do?"

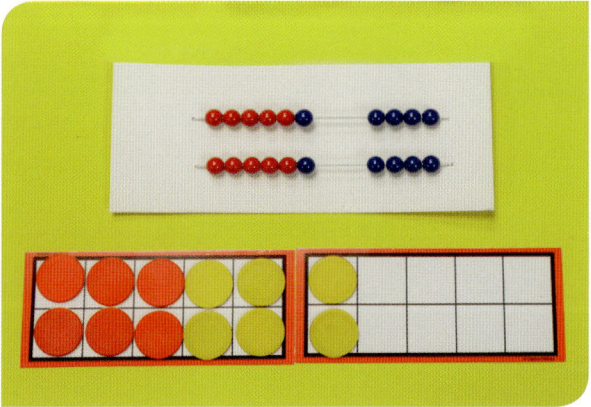

ARRAYS

Arrays are complex for young children to understand, but experience in constructing their own will help them to understand how they are made of equal rows and columns. The first step for many children will be making one row of 3, 4 or 5 items that are evenly spaced and then replicating it to make a row underneath. This is easiest to do with items that are the same size and shape. They can go on to make another row, and another and another.

Say what you see

I see 1, 2, 3 … 12.

I see 3 rows of 4.

If you go round the other side, it's 4 rows of 3.

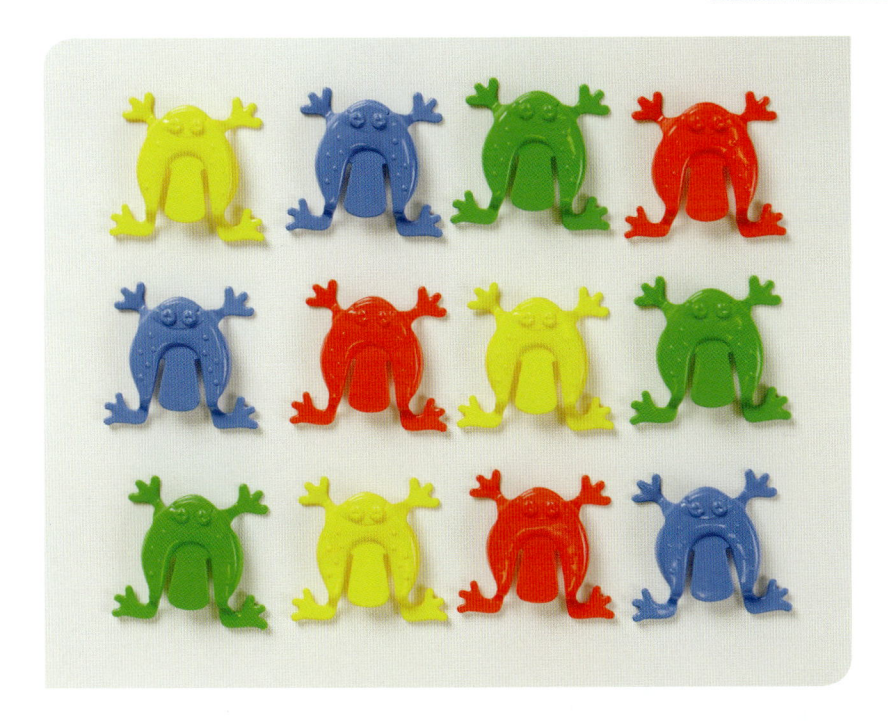

I see 4 and 4 and 4.

It's 3 and 3 and 3 and 3.

It's 4 trebled!

Research link:

Barmby, Harries and Higgins (2010) found that children aged six and seven had difficulty recognizing the array as a representation of multiplication and only about half of children aged eight and nine had this recognition.

3 Exploring 9 to 20

FINDING THE DIFFERENCE

Finding the difference, where two groups of objects are being compared, is more difficult than subtraction as 'taking away'. An interesting context will make it easier to understand and practical games like this provide repeated experiences to help children make connections.

The fish and worm game

You need 20 fish, 20 pipe cleaner worms and a dice or cards numbered 1 to 20.

Two children take it in turns to throw the dice (or pick a card), one making their number with fish and the other with 'worms'.

After playing the game for a while children can investigate how to check their answer on a calculator: they may not realize that to find the difference above they need to press '12 – 7 ='. Using the calculator to represent difference helps children to link the minus sign to other kinds of subtraction problems.

Later they can play this game with other manipulatives and develop the mathematical but tricky language of difference, including 'how many more?' alongside abstract representations like the number line.

Whenever we introduce a new idea to children, it helps to set it in a sensible context and to use numbers with which children are confident and comfortable. If the numbers are too big, the new idea will get lost as they have to pay too much attention to the numbers rather than the idea. This will still be important as we extend the range of numbers in the next chapter.

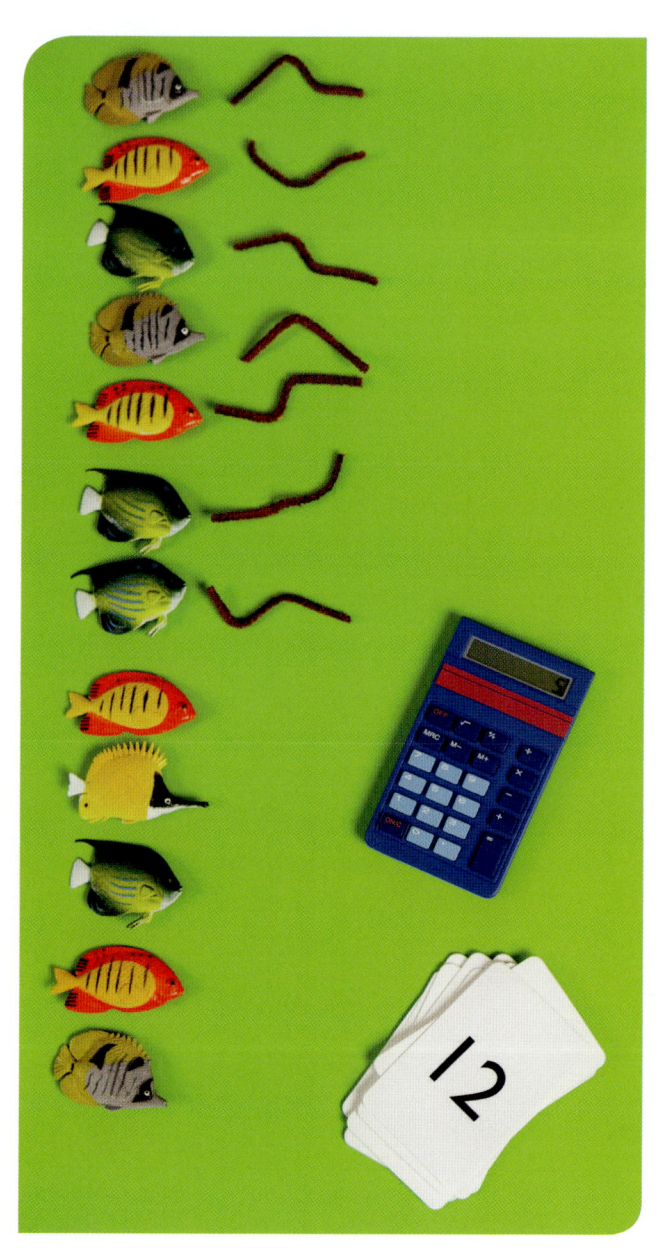

12 fish and 7 worms. How many fish won't get a worm? Or how many spare worms are there?

Chapter Four: Exploring 15 to 50

Fifty can seem like a very large number to children.

The aim of this chapter is to make numbers in this range familiar and manageable.

The number names follow a more predictable pattern once you know the decade number words: twenty, thirty, forty and fifty. Counting larger numbers of objects requires more organisation and so grouping becomes a key strategy. Groups of 2, 5 and 10 are especially important. Seeing a group of 10 as one 'ten' forms a vital part of children's understanding of our number system and using manipulatives will help to introduce ideas about place value.

In this chapter we build knowledge of addition and subtraction by looking at partitioning larger collections of items. We develop ideas about multiplying and dividing by counting objects in groups and making arrays.

How many toys?

4 Exploring 15 to 50

COUNTING BIGGER COLLECTIONS

Counting forwards and backwards helps children to become familiar with the number names to 50. To link these with the written symbols, children can generate the sequence by using a calculator and adding 1 again and again. They can then explore counting backwards by taking away 1 repeatedly.

Children need experience of counting larger collections of objects, with a choice of things they like to count. Many children will try to count larger numbers without a system and then realize that it is hard to keep track. Useful strategies include lining things up or moving them out of the way as you count.

Practising in pairs, children can work both ways round: sometimes asking their partner for a specific number of things and sometimes giving their partner a pile of things to count.

Initially, leave children to explore counting in their own way, so that they can discuss alternative strategies and come to their own conclusions about efficient ways of counting.

Holly and Nina were counting a set of 51 coloured lolly sticks and decided to count some each and then add the amounts to find the total. When Holly and Nina saw that William and Dinesh had grouped their conkers by putting them in tens, they decided that this would have been better.

Research link:

Sarama and Clements (2009) point out that the most successful way of teaching efficient methods for solving problems is to build on children's invented strategies.

Counting in twos

One way to speed up counting is to count in twos. As they have done with smaller numbers, children can start by counting a set of objects in ones and then count them again in twos to check they get the same answer. This will help to avoid the problem of children who know the oral sequence 2, 4, 6 … but do not always match the words with pairs of objects.

Of course, counting an even number of objects in twos is very straightforward. Children also need practice at counting odd numbers, so they are able to switch from counting in twos to counting the odd item at the end.

Odd or even?

One way of helping children to understand odd and even numbers between 20 and 50 is to ask them to investigate making pairs.

Amina and Max counted out 37 conkers and arranged them in pairs to see if 37 was odd or even. They said, "There is one left over so it must be odd." They then tried other numbers and circled the odd ones on their number line. When their teacher asked what they had noticed, Amina said, "All the odd numbers end with 1, 3, 5, 7 or 9." Max commented, "They go up in 2s."

Chapter Four: Exploring 15 to 50

4 Exploring 15 to 50

COUNTING IN FIVES

5 is a group that children can soon recognise easily, and it helps with counting bigger numbers too. Counting in fives means more than just reciting the number sequence: children need to connect this to counting objects grouped in 5s.

When they put items in rows of five, children can see the pattern "5, 10, 15 ..." more clearly.

Show your hands!

Try these three games with five children at the front of the class. To start with, children watching may need to count individual fingers but with practice they will realize that they can count in fives and get to the same answer.

- The five children put up hands in turn, starting with no hands up to 10 hands, and the class practise counting up and down in fives.
- On a count of 3, the five children show one, two or no hands – they can choose. This game generates a lot of excitement as the number can be so unpredictable, ranging between 0 and 50.
- Ask the five children to show a specific multiple of 5 and let them sort out the number of hands they need.

Making 'fives' can be a helpful way to build on the skills of counting up and back in fives. 5s can be made from strips of card or from interlocking cubes. Alternatively, use coloured rods.

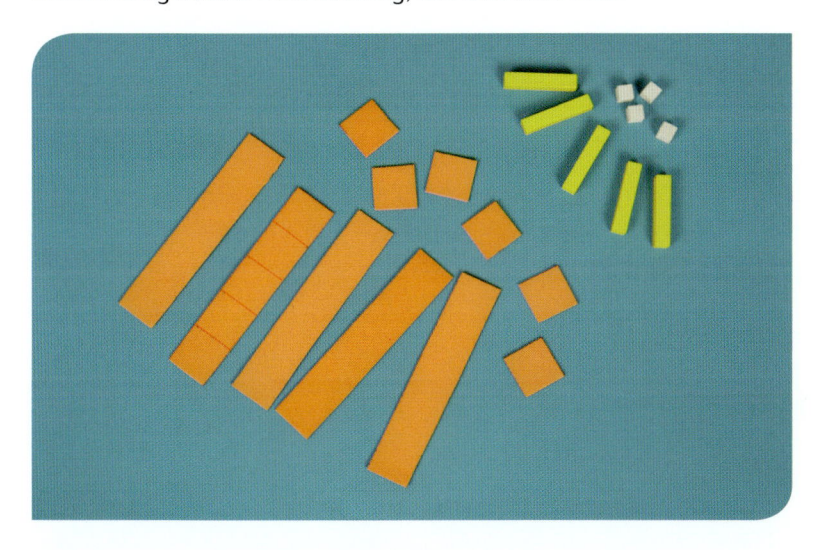

The Fives and Ones Game: What numbers can you make with just 5s?

Children work with a partner: one chooses a number between 0 and 50 and writes it down. Their partner says whether they think they can make it with just 5s or if they will need some ones as well. Then they make the number.

32 cannot be made with just 5s.

The children can make a list together of the numbers that they can make with just 5s. What do they notice? Let the children take it in turns to choose or make the numbers.

This activity helps children explore whether numbers have 5 as a factor (i.e. are multiples of 5). They can also investigate how many 5s are in particular numbers and discuss remainders.

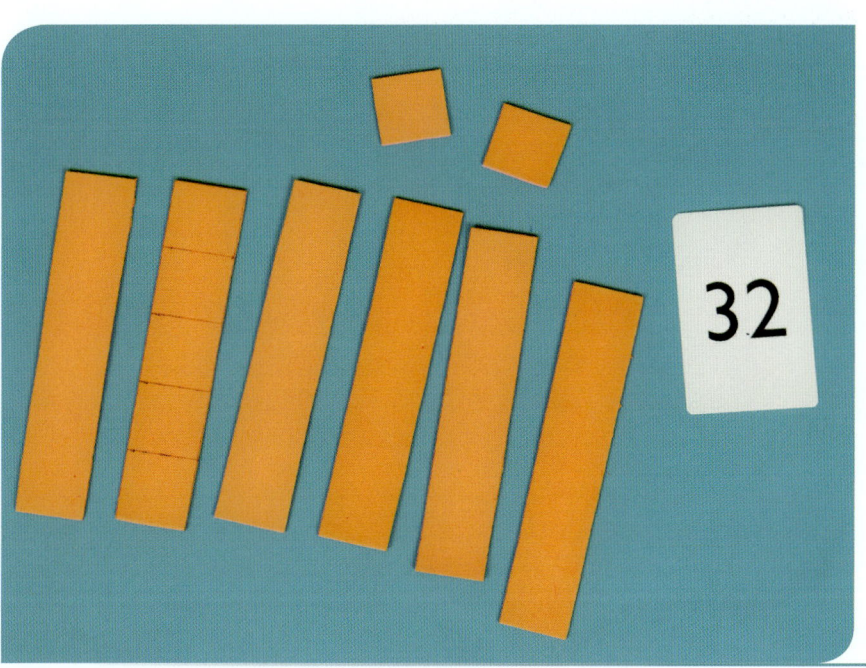

Chapter Four: Exploring 15 to 50

4 Exploring 15 to 50

SAYING AND WRITING NUMBERS TO 50

In our number system, the *place* of each digit within a number, tells you its *value*. For example, in the number 42, the value of the digit 4 is 40 (or 4 tens), whereas in the number 24 the digit 4 is worth 4 ones.

However, children often find it difficult to distinguish between numbers like thirteen and thirty because they sound so similar. Sometimes they will also struggle to write the digits in the correct order and will mix up 13 and 31.

Arnie (aged seven) was putting numbers on an empty number line to twenty. When asked, "Where will fifteen go?" he laughed and said, "but fifteen is more than 20!" Arnie seemed to be confusing fifteen with fifty, although he clearly said "fifteen."

Place value cards combined with resources can help children clarify this confusion.

Show children 13, 30 and 31 made with place value cards and ask them to make the numbers: "How do you know which number this is? What is the same and what is different?"

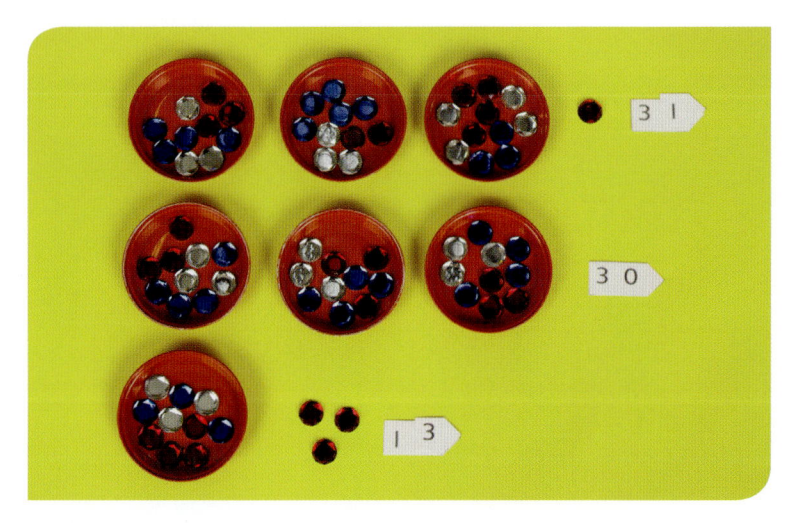

Repeat the activity with 15, 50 and 51 or 14, 40 and 41.

Children can consolidate these ideas by writing labels for groups they have counted. When they are uncertain, they can check numbers on a number line.

STICKS IN ORDER

Lolly sticks are useful manipulatives for comparing the sizes of numbers.

Three or four children can play this game with place value cards for 10, 20, 30 and 40, and all the numbers from 1 to 9. They should spread the cards on the table face down to start.

Children take it in turns to pick up a tens card and a ones card, make a number and show it with lolly sticks. Some children may want to count individual sticks, or they can bundle some of the sticks in tens ready to play.

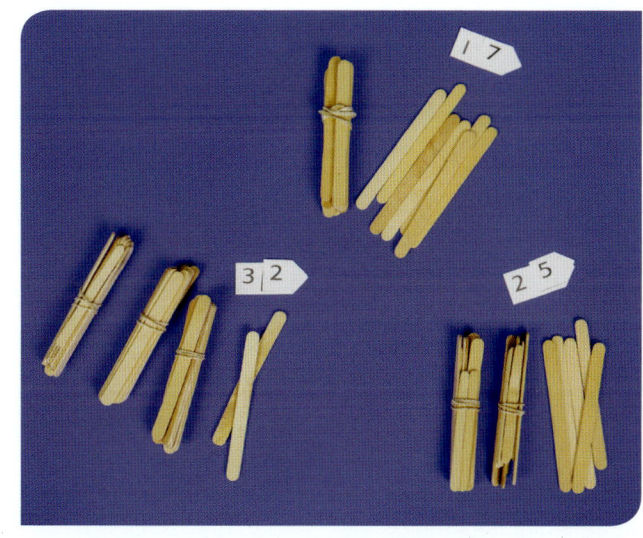

Can you put the numbers in order, smallest to biggest?

Children can play the game several times. They can vary the game by putting the numbers in order from biggest to smallest.

Here are two ways that children could record what they have found out:

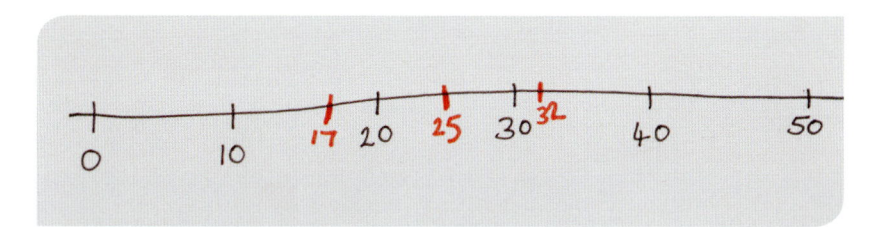

Write the three numbers on a number line labelled with 0, 10, 20, 30, 40 and 50.

17 is smallest then 25 then 32
17 < 25 < 32

Write the numbers in order and put in the signs for smaller than < or bigger than >.

Chapter Four: Exploring 15 to 50

63

4 Exploring 15 to 50

HALF A HUNDRED HEDGEHOGS

Making things from salt dough is very appealing to young children and hedgehogs are creatures with which many children are familiar.

The hedgehogs shown here are from a 3-minute animation called 'Half a Hundred Hedgehogs', available on *Oxford Owl*. You can use the animation as an introduction to a lesson, for children to watch at home or as a model for classroom activity that follows a similar pattern using your own hedgehogs.

Recipe for salt dough (to make about 50 hedgehogs):

- 1 mug of cooking salt
- 2 mugs of plain flour
- a dessert spoon of cooking oil
- just under a mug of cold water.

1 Mix the salt and flour together, add oil, tip in three quarters of the cold water then mix together. Keep adding a little more water at a time until the dough stays together – but you don't want it too sticky!

2 Make little balls of dough, then pat into a hedgehog shape (directly onto a baking sheet, if possible). Use a pencil to make two holes for the eyes, and sideways marks for the spines.

3 Bake for about an hour and a half / two hours at 120 degrees Celsius, until dry and hard.

4 When cool, use a black felt pen to mark eyes and a nose.

Once children have made lots of hedgehogs they will be keen to count them. Can they make half a hundred?

Chapter Four: Exploring 15 to 50

65

4 Exploring 15 to 50

GROUPS WITHIN 50

50 items in a random arrangement are difficult to count and it is hard to know whether you have them all. Helping children to find different ways of organizing 50 will encourage them to see the links between addition and subtraction, multiplication and division.

Talking about the idea of a *number* of 10s is very sophisticated. This is described in the research literature as *unitizing*. For those who are grappling with counting in ones, to treat ten things as one thing, and to talk about 'a ten', may seem contradictory. Similarly, thinking about 50 as ten 5s involves unitizing, i.e. seeing five separate items as one lot of five.

5 rows of 10.

Making 10s, making 5s

Children can use their own hedgehogs, pebbles, conkers or small toys to experiment with arranging them in 10s and 5s. Ask them to talk about what they have done, to look at other children's arrangements and to say what they see.

Encourage children to write as many number sentences as they can to show what they can see. It helps to discuss the fact that, in this context, the multiplication sign is a very condensed way of expressing 'lots of'.

Research link:

Wright, Stanger, Stafford and Martland (2014) note that unitizing is a major development in children's multiplicative thinking. For example, a child who can unitize can think abstractly in terms of repeated 3s, or answering "How many 3s make 18?"

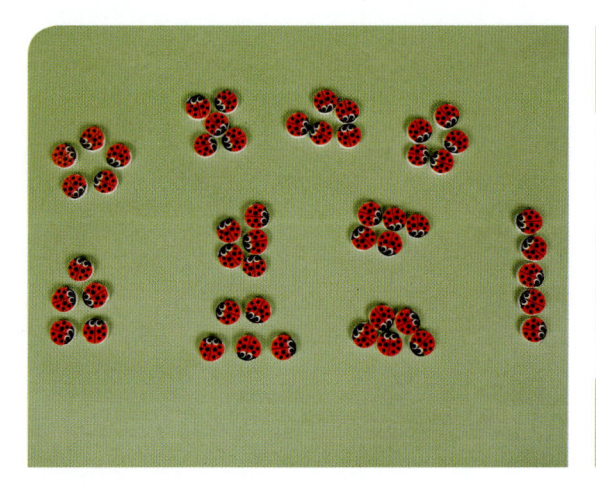

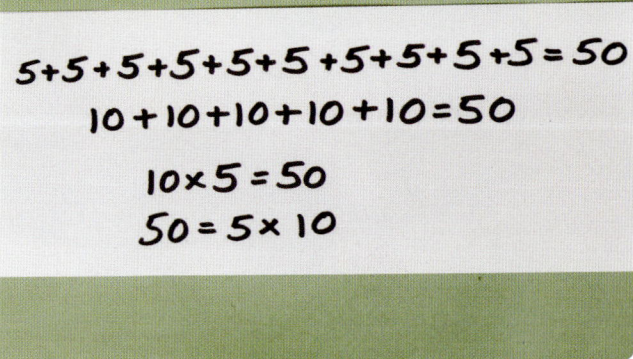

$5+5+5+5+5+5+5+5+5+5=50$

$10+10+10+10+10=50$

$10 \times 5 = 50$

$50 = 5 \times 10$

Halving 50

Halving is an idea that children readily understand. Children can start by choosing from the numbers 20, 30, 40 and 50 and finding half. This will build their knowledge of important doubling facts such as 15 + 15 = 30. They can then choose other numbers under 50 to halve. Finding out which ones leave a remainder is another way of identifying odd and even numbers.

Which group should the last hedgehog join?

Making 2s

Even when children have seen someone else demonstrate that twenty-five 2s make 50, it is useful for them to do this themselves. It may surprise children that both halving 50 and asking "How many 2s in 50?" give the answer of 25.

Division can be seen as sharing or grouping. Halving 50 is the same as sharing it between 2 whereas finding how many 2s make 50 is the same as grouping in 2s. If children want to use a calculator, both of these are solved by keying in 50 ÷ 2 =. Using the calculator is a good way of introducing the division symbol.

An array like this is useful to help children see how halving and grouping are linked. Exploring this connection with other examples and explaining to each other will help them to understand this relationship.

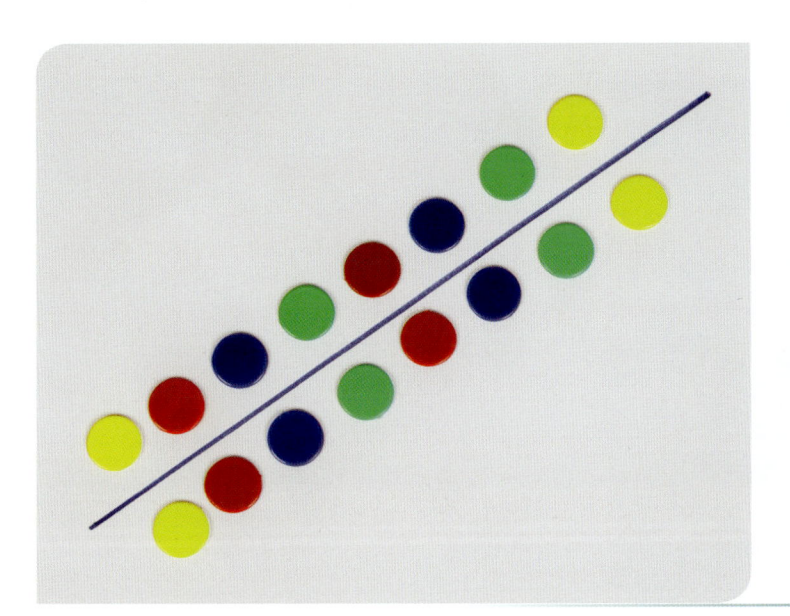

How many 2s in 16? It's 8!

What is half of 16? It's 8!

Can you see why they are the same?

Chapter Four: Exploring 15 to 50

67

4   Exploring 15 to 50

50 IN TENS

Looking at a group of ten in different ways helps to build the idea of 'a ten' and more than one 'ten'. Children love counting up in tens because they can reach big numbers quickly; counting back is important as well.

Five ways of showing 10 hedgehogs.

Mega facts

The number bonds to 50 in whole tens can be seen as an extension of the number facts to 5. Children are excited to see that because 1 + 4 = 5, they know a 'mega fact' that 10 + 40 = 50. Later they will realize that 100 + 400 = 500 and 1 million add 4 million makes 5 million.

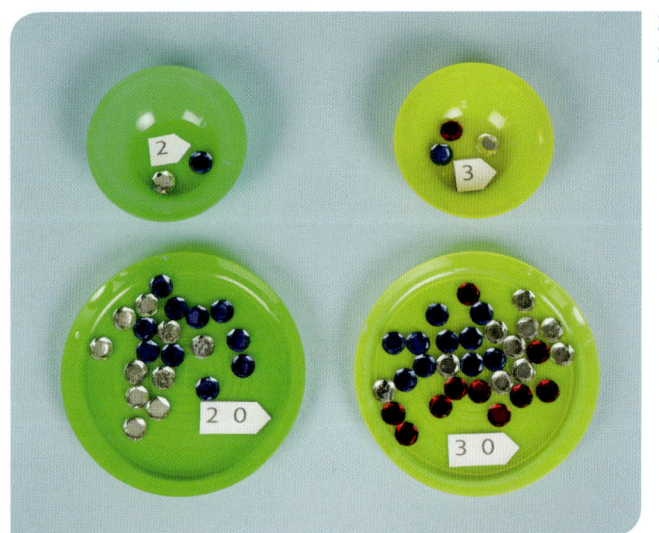

2 + 3 = 5 so
20 + 30 = 50.

Tens and bead strings

Using 50 of the beads on a bead string, children can show as many ways of splitting 50 in tens as they can find. They can talk about what they see in terms of numbers of tens.

Give the children the opportunity to experiment and create their own statements and number sentences like these:

20 and 20 and 10 makes 50
50 is 4 lots of 10 and 10 more
50 − 20 = 30
20 + 10 = 50 − 20
10 = 50 − 40

Hiding Hedgehogs

Children can count or use facts they know to work out the missing number. Start by using multiples of ten, then multiples of five and then any number within 50 for the hidden number. For variety use other animals and different places to hide them.

There are 50 hedgehogs altogether. How many are hiding in the box?

Chapter Four: Exploring 15 to 50

69

4 Exploring 15 to 50

MAKING ARRAYS

Arrays are a powerful representation of multiplication. Children need lots of practice with making and describing their own arrays.

When children are making arrays they must make sure that each row has the same number, each column has the same number and they are spaced evenly.

Children can start with rows of 5, adding row after row until they get as close as they can to 50.

3 rows of 5 are 15.

Each row gives you 5 more. 5, 10, 15, 20, 25, 30.

If you turn it round you can see 5 lots of 6 are 30.

I can see three 5s and three 5s.

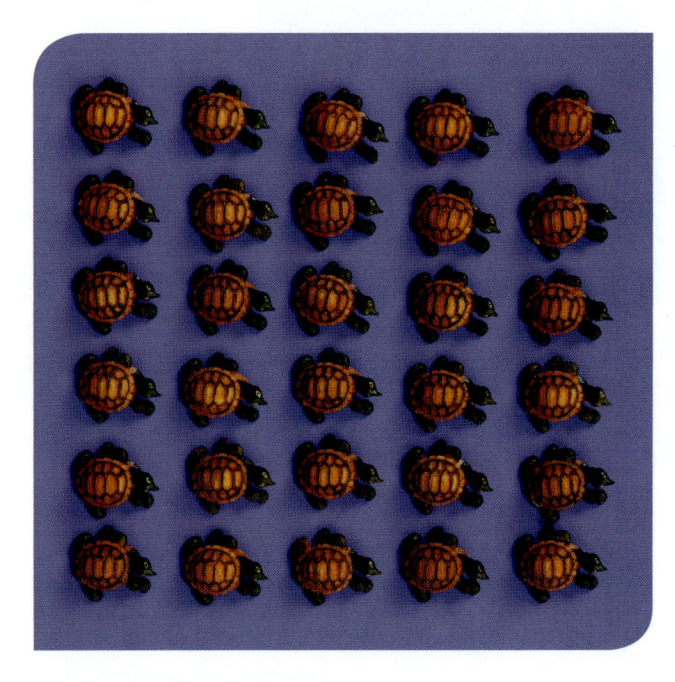

Each column has 6 in it.

There are 6 rows altogether so I can see 6 lots of 5 are 30.

If you want 20 you need 4 rows of 5.

This array shows 5 columns of 6 as well as 6 rows of 5: multiplication is commutative. Children may need to turn the array round to see the multiples of six: 6, 12, 18, 24, 30. This will be easier if the array has been laid out on card.

Arrays can be used to build any times table. A sensible order is to work with 2s, 5s and 10s up to 10 rows and then 3s, 4s and 6s.

Research link:

Bobis, Mulligan and Lowrie (2013) found that children had difficulties in recognizing and understanding arrays and that plenty of experience with constructing them helped to develop children's awareness of their pattern and structure.

Arrays and factors

Children can investigate the different arrays they can make with a number of counters that they choose. Good numbers to explore include 18, 21, 24 and 25. Children may be surprised to learn that an array can have just one row!

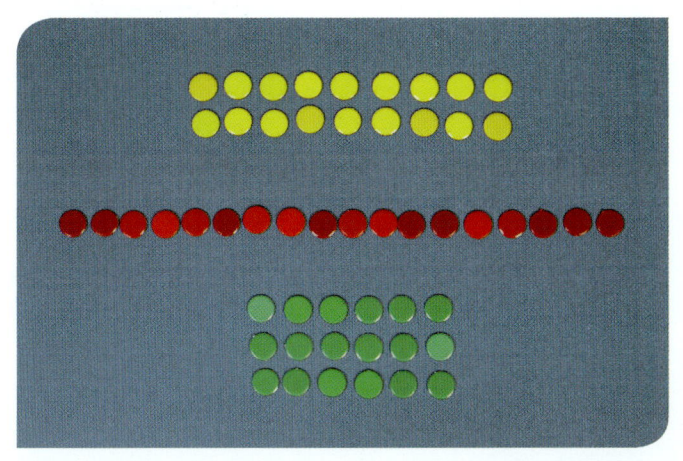

Here are the arrays you can make with 18

When children have found all the arrays they can make for a number, they can see all the numbers that 'go into' it exactly. For 18, these are 1, 2, 3, 6, 9 and 18 and we call them the factors of 18. Factors help us to see linked multiplication and division facts: for example 3 × 6 = 18 so 6 = 18 ÷ 3.

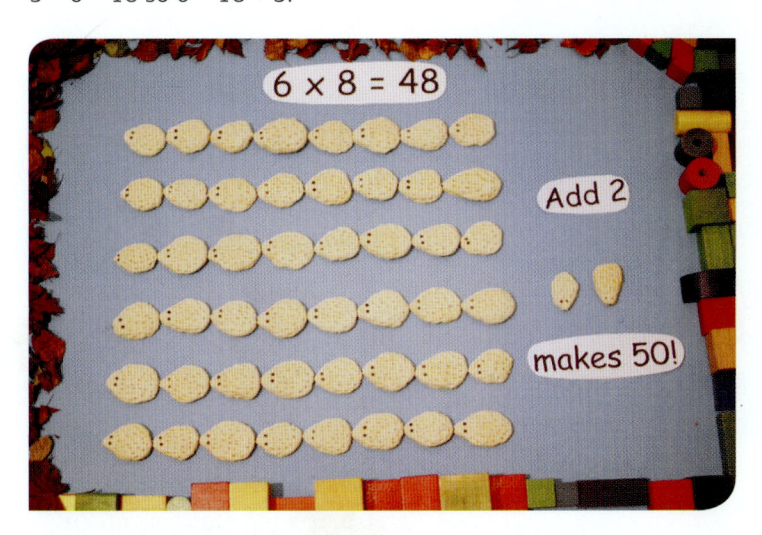

Not every number goes into every other number! For example you cannot make 50 with just 6s or just 8s. The closest we can get to 50 with 6s or 8s is 48: we have a remainder of 2 hedgehogs.

4 Exploring 15 to 50

SAME LENGTH TRAINS

Coloured number rods are a significant resource for exploring factors of numbers, by making 'trains' of the same length with just one colour of rod. For children who are unfamiliar with the value of the rods, it helps to start by building a staircase from 1 to 10 to refer to.

Start with a number under 20 to establish the principles involved. We have chosen 15 as an example.

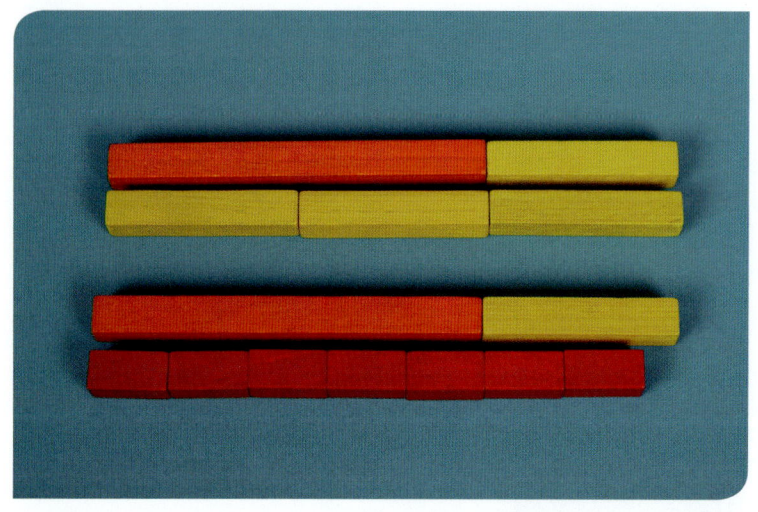

I made a train of the same length with 5s – the yellow rods. I tried with 2s – the red rods – but it didn't work.

Using the rods helps the child to see that you can make 15 with three 5s but you cannot make it with 2s. This example shows that 5 is a factor of 15 but 2 is not.

Research link:

Goutard (1964) developed a very successful approach to teaching arithmetic with young children using Cuisenaire rods. She also encouraged children to visualize the rods, talk about what they had found and then record what they had found in their own way.

As children move on to making trains for bigger numbers, they will gradually realize that it helps to try out the numbers in order: 1s, 2s, 3s, etc.

In the example below, the child has separated out the numbers that work from the ones that do not.

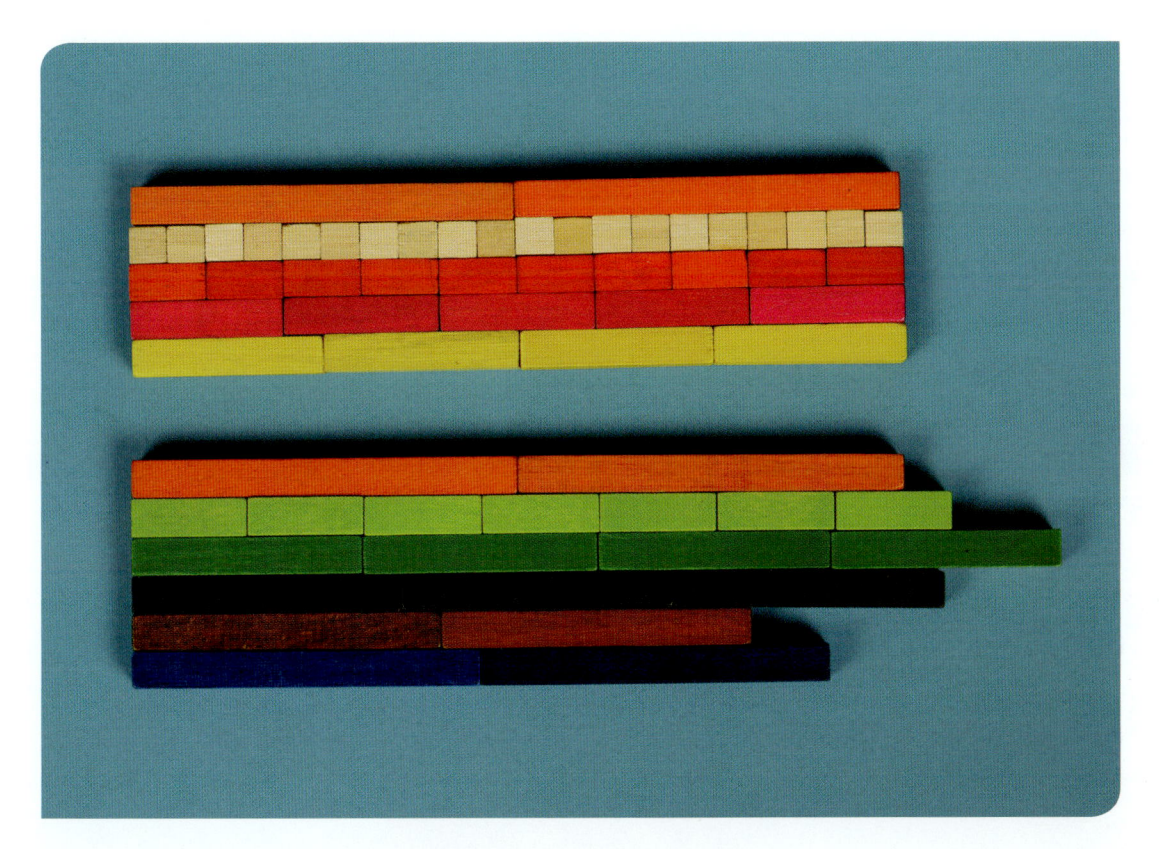

You can make 20 with 1s, 2s, 4s, and 5s so they are factors of 20. You can't make 20 with the others so 3, 6, 7, 8 and 9 are not factors of 20.

4 Exploring 15 to 50

LOLLY STICKS AND STORIES

Stories are a good starting point to help children make sense of addition and subtraction. A story should give a context that children can imagine, deciding whether they should add or subtract. The answer is not the only point of engaging children this way: using manipulatives supports children in developing strategies and explaining what they have done.

It is good for children to see that they can solve a variety of problems with the same equipment. Here we have used individual items grouped in 10s, which children can check for themselves and take apart if they wish.

Jack wants to collect all 44 model figures in the set. He has got 26 so far. How many more would he need?

Afia used a *counting up strategy*. She took 2 bundles of 10 lolly sticks and 6 loose ones, making 26. She then got 4 more to make 30 and another bundle of 10 to make 40. Then she collected 4 more. Then she said 4 and 10 and 4 makes 18.

Eliza used a *partitioning strategy*. She collected 44 sticks in 4 bundles of 10 and 4 separate sticks. She took away 2 bundles of 10. Then she said, "I need 6 more to make 26: that's this 4 but then I need another 2." She split one bundle of 10 and took 2. She said, "That leaves 8 and this last bundle of 10 so Jack needs 18 more."

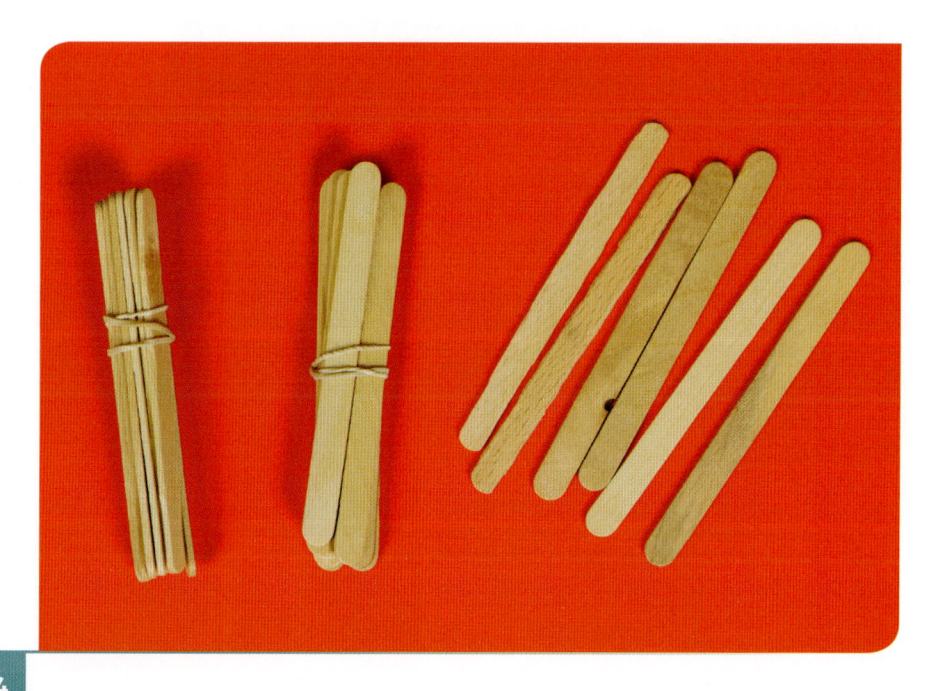

Today, in Mrs Khan's class, 12 children have packed lunches, 17 children have school dinners and three children go home for lunch. How many children are here today?

Riyad used *partitioning*. He said, "I collected together the 10s and had 20 and then added together the others: 2 and 7 and 3 is 12 and with the 20 that means there are 32 children altogether."

Layla spotted a *number fact* she knew. She said, "I put 17 sticks and 3 sticks together because that makes 20. With the extra 12 that's 32."

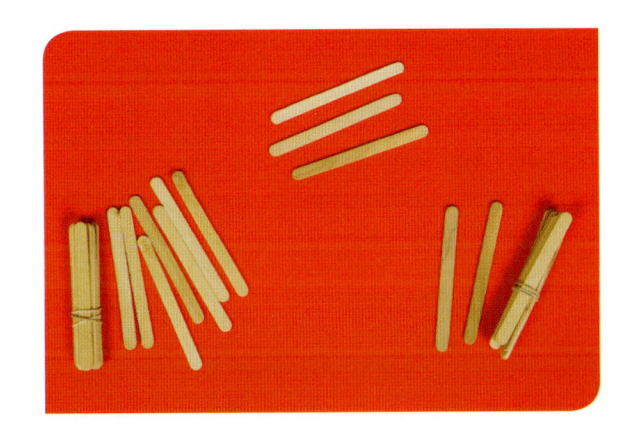

Kyla had a packet of 36 birthday candles. She used up 17 for her big sister's birthday last week. How many candles has she got left?

Ethan and Sasha both used a *taking away strategy* but did it slightly differently.

Ethan said, "I took away a bundle of 10 and then the 6 but that wasn't enough so I undid another bundle and took 1 more. There are 19 left."

Sasha said, "I did it a different way. I took two bundles of 10 but that was 3 too many so I put those back with the others. There are 19 left."

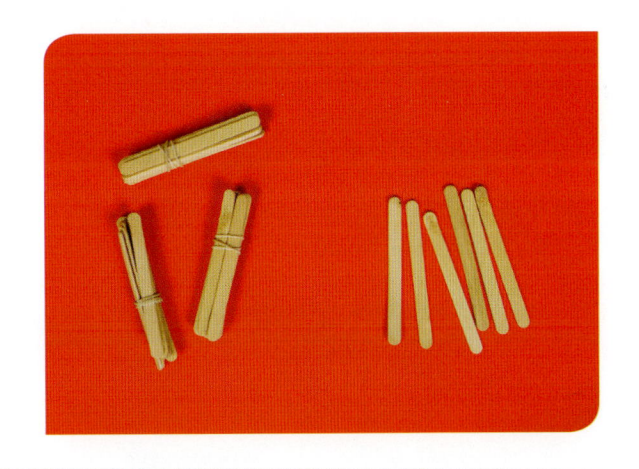

Watching and listening to children working in this way gives teachers vital information about children's thinking and understanding.

4 Exploring 15 to 50

USING WHAT YOU KNOW

Bead strings grouped in 10s can be useful manipulatives for deriving related facts and spotting the patterns. Children need to notice first of all that you can see 'a ten' even when the beads are not all the same colour.

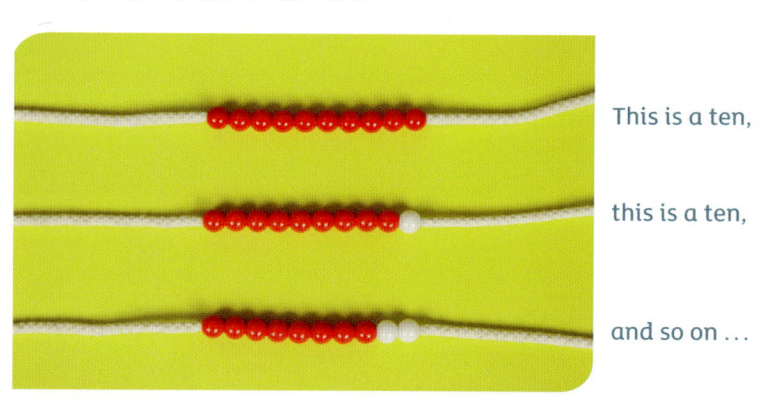

This is a ten,

this is a ten,

and so on ...

Make new facts by adding whole tens to start with.

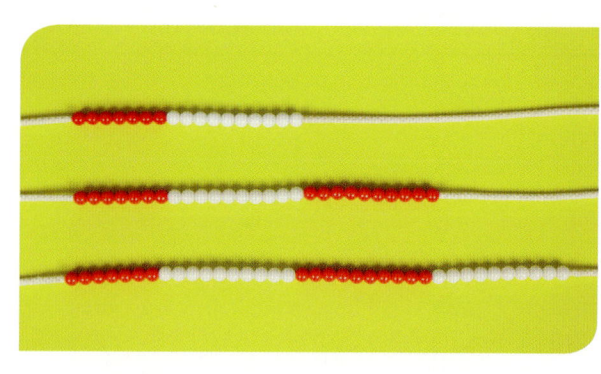

If you know 7 + 10 = 17,

then you can see 7 + 20 = 27,

and 7 + 30 = 37.

This can also be linked to related subtractions such as 27 − 20 = 7 and 27 − 7 = 20.

Children can go on to spot patterns when adding a single-digit number to any 2-digit number.

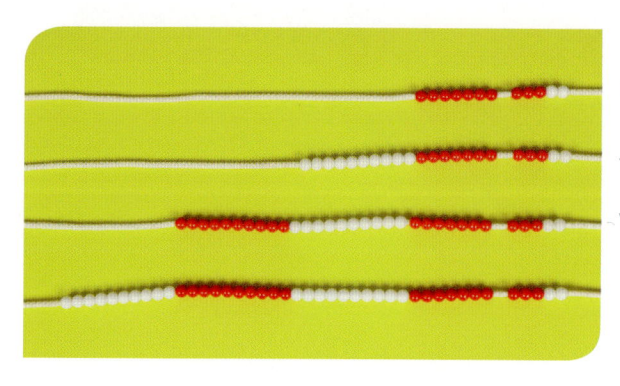

If you know 7 + 5 = 12,

then you can see 17 + 5 = 22.

What else can you make?

Once again children can link these to related subtraction facts.

Complements of 50

When children know the number bonds to 10, they can use these to find complements to 50: in other words how many more they need to make 50.

Using the bead string helps children avoid the common mistake of thinking that 34 + 26 = 50 because they can see that one of the tens is split.

When children are confident in showing relationships on bead strings, they will be able to use a number line with understanding.

4 + 6 makes 10 so to 34 + 6 = 40 and 34 + 16 = 50.

34

Chapter Four: Exploring 15 to 50

4 Exploring 15 to 50

THE ANT TIMES TABLE

Jane's class were learning the six times table.

The children worked in pairs at first. They used a 0 to 5 dice and a little pile of plastic ants. One child threw the dice; they counted out that many ants and worked out how many legs they had altogether. Phoenix and Nita laughed when they threw zero: "No ants – no legs! No sixes makes none!"

Next, the children worked with the table in order, laying out ants and working out the number of legs.

Finally, the children chose a tables fact and drew ants – or other insects – to show how many legs they would have. Jane encouraged them to think about what else they could figure out from their drawings – using the plastic ants if that helped them.

$0 \times 6 = 0$
$1 \times 6 = 6$
$2 \times 6 = 12$
$3 \times 6 = 18$
$4 \times 6 = 24$
$5 \times 6 = 30$
$6 \times 6 = 36$

$3 \times 6 = 18$
$18 = 6 \times 3$

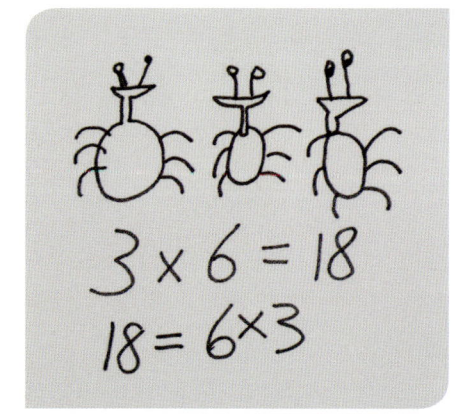

Jess chose to illustrate 3 × 6 = 18, and knew that 6 × 3 was the same, as she said, "3 ants with 6 legs; 6 legs each on 3 ants, it's the same."

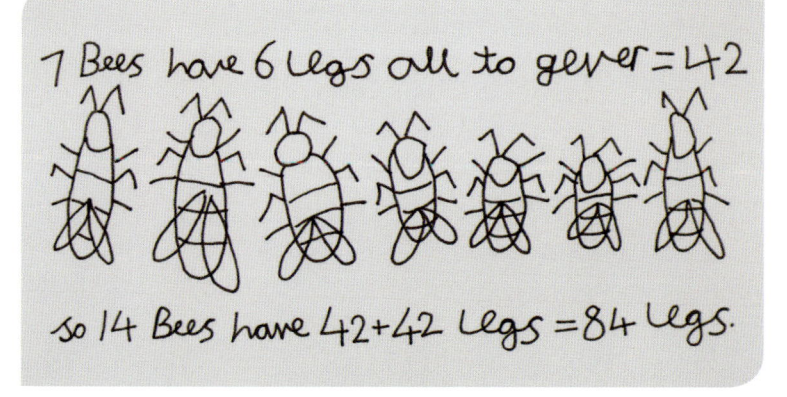

7 Bees have 6 legs all together = 42
so 14 Bees have 42+42 legs = 84 legs.

Ria used the fact that double 7 is 14 to extend her tables fact beyond ten 6s.

Children who feel confident that they understand what they are doing will soon begin to be more ambitious than you might expect! The next chapter extends our range of numbers further, concentrating especially on one hundred.

Chapter Five: Exploring 25 to 200 and beyond

Children's confidence with tens and hundreds can grow very quickly when it is built on a good understanding of smaller numbers.

Counting is a very important element of working with larger numbers; children need practice at counting in ones up to one hundred and beyond, and back down to zero, starting at any number in the sequence. However, counting in ones has disadvantages when we deal with larger and larger numbers. It takes a long time and that means we are more likely to make mistakes. Our number system is based on multiples of ten (because of our fingers – a handy calculating aid!), so grouping things in tens is a sensible and efficient way of finding out how many we have.

Grouping ten 10s to make one hundred is a significant step forward. Time spent concentrating on the size of 100 will make children feel more confident that this is a number they can imagine or visualize – an important part of being able to estimate and to work with a number mentally.

Using tens and ones together, not just ones, helps us be quicker and more accurate with bigger numbers. Of course, we could answer a sum such as 36 + 45 by counting out 36 single items, then 45 items, then counting up how many there are altogether. One more efficient way might be to think of 30 and 40, 6 and 5, and add those together. A good knowledge of how numbers combine will also provide children with several other ways they could solve this addition.

In this chapter we extend ideas of counting, comparison and composition to build children's confidence in the four arithmetical operations with numbers to 200.

5 Exploring 25 to 200

COUNTING TO 100

Fortunately, the decade numbers beyond fifty are closely linked to numbers six, seven, eight and nine, so children can learn the numbers from sixty to ninety-nine quite quickly. They will still need plenty of practice counting backwards – and to count up and down starting from any number from 1 to 100.

Fifty pence

Before moving on to larger numbers, you might want to check some children's counting to 50 by asking them to give you the right number of pennies to swap for a fifty pence piece. Encourage them to put the pennies in neat rows of ten, as this helps others to check they have counted correctly.

Count up, count down

Children can practise counting forwards and backwards with a partner, using a 50 pence piece, 49 pennies and the cards numbered 50 to 99 from a pack of 100.

Each child takes a card. The child with the smaller number counts out that much money, starting with the 50 pence piece. Then their partner has to count out loud forwards from there, adding a penny for each number, until they have reached the bigger number.

After a few turns at counting forwards, they can work backwards: count out the bigger number, then take away a penny at a time, counting out loud until they get down to the smaller number.

Children will enjoy using real coins as an alternative to play money whenever possible.

Jess and Nino counted backwards from 92 to 86.

Making a hundred

Children can begin to get a better sense of the size of one hundred if they help make collections of 100 items. You can announce a 'total so far' each day, and work out how many more you need to make 100.

Ready-made hundreds can get you started. For example, a bag of 100 cotton wool balls, 100 drinking straws or a notepad with 100 pages. There might be 100 of some items in your classroom that can go on display for a while like 100 pencils, or 100 plastic cubes. Children may be able to collect natural items such as shells, acorns and pine cones, or objects from home such as plastic milk bottle tops, postcards, badges or old keys.

They can also draw or make 100 things, such as 100 snails, 100 paper snakes or 100 woolly spiders. Talk about how many each child would need to collect or make: "There are 30 children in our class. If everyone made two snakes, how many would we have? What if everyone made three? How many more would we need to make 100?"

5 Exploring 25 to 200

TEN TENS AND A DRAGON

Has the dragon got 100 pom-poms?

The dragon in this story is keen to make collections of 100. A story context is another way of helping children make sense of mathematics – it is not a real-life problem, but an imaginary one, where things still need to be organized in a systematic way.

The scenes shown here are from a 4-minute animation called 'Ten Tens and a Dragon', available on *Oxford Owl*. You can use the animation as an introduction to a lesson, for children to watch at home and as a model for classroom activity that follows a similar pattern, using your own items. You can show the animation several times, pausing whenever you want to discuss a section with children.

Working with collections of 100 items helps children to think about several ideas:

- counting up to 100 (and back again) in ones, fives and tens
- how a number track can be made into a hundred square
- putting items into an array and showing that ten 10s make 100
- grouping in 10s where you can still see and count each ten
- grouping in 10s where the ten objects are hidden so you have to imagine them
- how to use the number facts you know, to derive other number facts
- using a variety of strategies for addition and subtraction within 100.

Number track to hundred square

Many diagrams in mathematics are mystifying to children, whilst they seem obvious to adults. The hundred square is one of these. It is important to show children how it is made, not just to present it as a finished item. They will then be able to use it as a model that helps them develop a greater range of mental methods.

A number track can be used to count small items, and matching one pom-pom to each number helps the dragon see that there are 100. However, a long number track is hard to handle, so cutting it into rows of ten provides us with a more convenient format: a hundred square. This representation of one hundred also opens up the opportunity to see several patterns in the numbers.

Children can work in pairs or threes to make strips of ten numbers on squared card: making 1 to 10, then 11 to 20, and so on. Show how these fit together to make a number track from 1 to 100, and how they can be moved to make a hundred square instead.

Children can then experiment with adding and taking away using counters or other small items on the hundred square, particularly to see what happens when you add or subtract ten (or 20, or 30). They can also see how useful it is to split the number you are adding or taking away, according to how many are needed to reach the next ten and beyond (sometimes called 'bridging through ten').

Nikola and Torin showed that you can do 37 + 5 by doing 37 + 3 + 2.

Research link:

Cobb (1995) emphasized the need to develop meaningful interpretations of images if they are to be used to support mathematical thinking. He describes a child who could not add 'a ten' on a hundred square because 'a ten' as an idea related to this image simply did not make sense to him.

5 Exploring 25 to 200

TEN TENS ARE ONE HUNDRED

When children are laying out an array, they will usually work horizontally, and put out one row of objects at a time. Dragon takes a different view, and puts up one column – a string of pom-poms – at a time. Many children will notice that Dragon has made a pattern across the ten by ten array, by threading colours in the same order each time.

Children can use 100 counters, shells, cubes or any other small objects to experiment with different ways of arranging 100, still using rows and columns but changing the spacing between them. For example, children could separate their items into five 20s or 70 and 30. Square dotty paper is useful to record what they find out.

What other ways can you find of arranging 100?

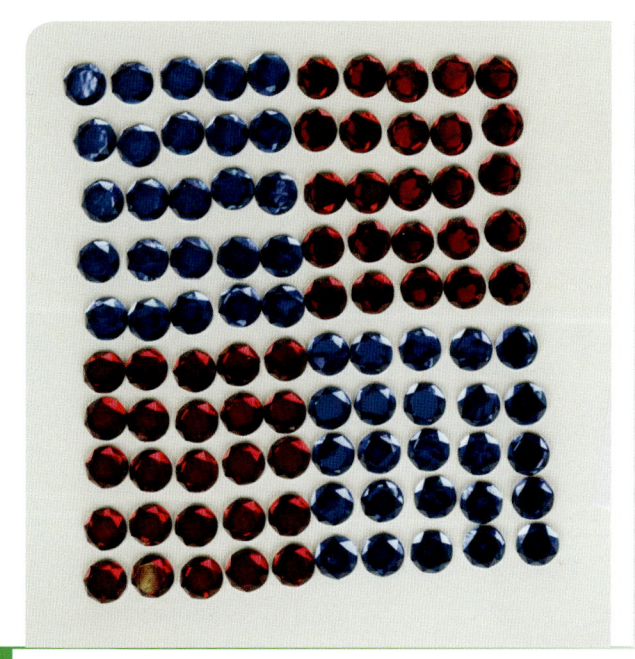

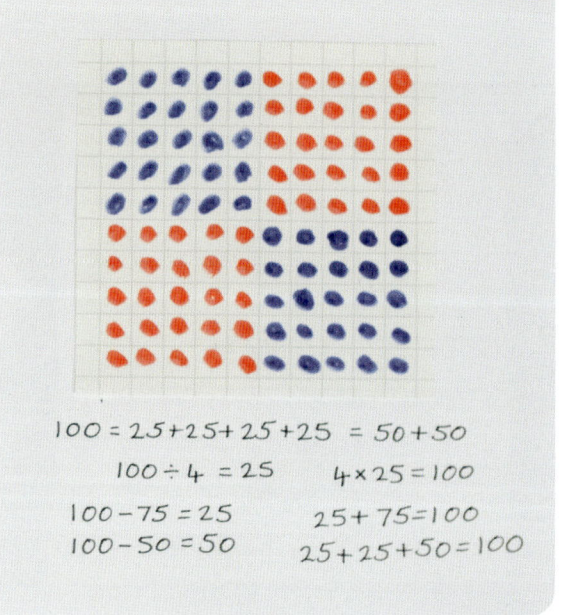

$$100 = 25 + 25 + 25 + 25 = 50 + 50$$
$$100 \div 4 = 25 \qquad 4 \times 25 = 100$$
$$100 - 75 = 25 \qquad 25 + 75 = 100$$
$$100 - 50 = 50 \qquad 25 + 25 + 50 = 100$$

Twenty lots of five

Plastic pegs and a ten by ten board provide an easy way to make arrays where everything lines up neatly. Alternatively, using counters and squared paper will keep things in line. Children can work with a partner, discuss what they can see, and think of ideas they can investigate.

Think about how you could make 100 with 5s. 100 is twenty 5s; 100 = 20 × 5.

Here are some more ideas to explore:

> Two 5s make 10; ten 10s make 100; Twenty 5s make 100.
>
> Two 5s make 10; eight 10s make 80; how many 5s make 80?
>
> Two 5s make 10; seven 10s make 70; how many 5s make 70?

> How many more 5s do you need to make 100, if you have ten 5s?
>
> If you have fifteen 5s?
>
> If you have five 5s?
>
> If you have seventeen 5s?

> Fourteen 5s are 70.
> Sixteen 5s are 80.
> What do you notice?
> What are eighteen 5s?

> Can you make 100 just with 15s?
> Can you make 100 with 20s?
> What about 30s?

Chapter Five: Exploring 25 to 200

85

5 Exploring 25 to 200

MAKING AND BREAKING GROUPS OF TEN

Putting ten items in a container is a convenient way of grouping them so that they do not need to be counted separately, but can be thought of as 'a ten'. Dragon counts up one hundred bells by making ten lots of ten this way. Children can do the same, using plant pot saucers, coffee lids or muffin cases with any small countable items. Separate containers help children see many more combinations of tens than putting ten in each compartment of an egg tray, for example, as they can regroup them in the way Dragon does.

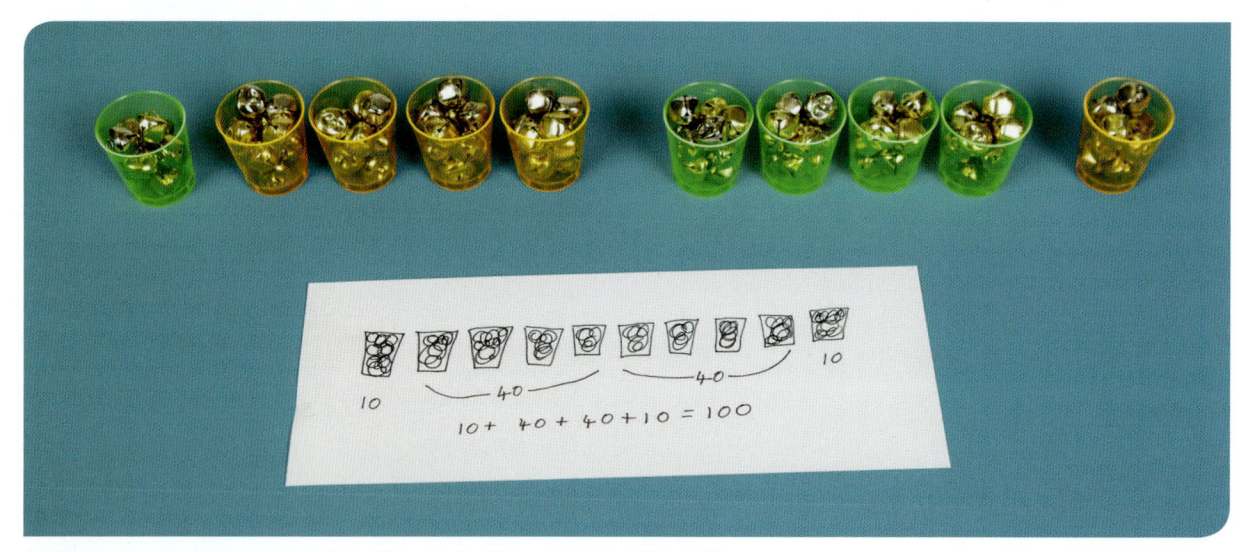

Children can make up questions for each other, such as "30 add 10 add 20 add something makes 100. What's the something?"

Counting more than 100

Working in a pair, children can start with ten groups of ten, then add further tens as they become more confident, extending their counting to 110, 120, 130 and so on. Encouraging them to count the first few numbers after 100 out loud in ones will help the surprising number of children who find it difficult to count across 100. Some will need practice in counting from 99 to 120 in ones.

Children can find 'mega facts' (like those in Chapter 4), relating what they know about numbers to 20 with their practical experience of bigger numbers.

TAKING AWAY SMALL NUMBERS

Counting backwards from 100 (or any other multiple of ten) needs practice. Counting backwards is a useful technique when you are subtracting one or two from a number, but can become unreliable if you try to take away larger numbers. In Dragon's story, the sheep takes three bells away from the hundred. Ask children to figure out how many that would leave. There are several sensible ways of calculating what is left. Children can use the equipment to show the methods they used, pointing or moving things as they explain.

Sundip said: "I counted back as I took them away: 99, 98, 97."

Grace used a number fact that she knew: "I could see it was 90 and some more. I know that 7 and 3 makes ten, so it must be 97 left."

Children may use other strategies when they are subtracting slightly larger numbers: this is what happened when their teacher asked children to calculate 100 – 6.

Eva liked counting in fives: "I thought it would be 95 if you took off 5, then you need another 1 to come off. It's 94."

Zack preferred working in tens: "It's going to be 90-something. 10 take away 6 is 4, so it's 94."

Children can work in pairs, taking turns to make up problems for each other and discussing ways of solving them. When they feel confident with taking away from 100, they can extend their range to 110 or 120.

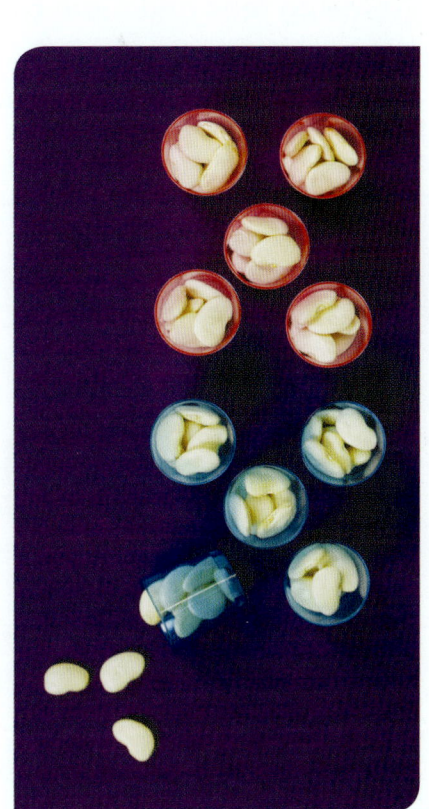

5 Exploring 25 to 200

COINS IN TENS AND ONES

Grouping items into tens that can no longer be seen, but need to be imagined, is a step further towards abstraction. Dragon puts ten coins in each of ten small boxes. The boxes of ten can be used to count out amounts very quickly.

Tens and ones

Working with place value cards and equipment together helps children find effective mental methods of completing a calculation.

There are several ways in which this calculation can be done. One common method is to do 20 + 30 then 3 + 8, then add 50 and 11 to get 61. Children can discuss other ways they could find the total. For example, Kodi told his teacher he would do 38 + 20 makes 58, then add 3 to make 61.

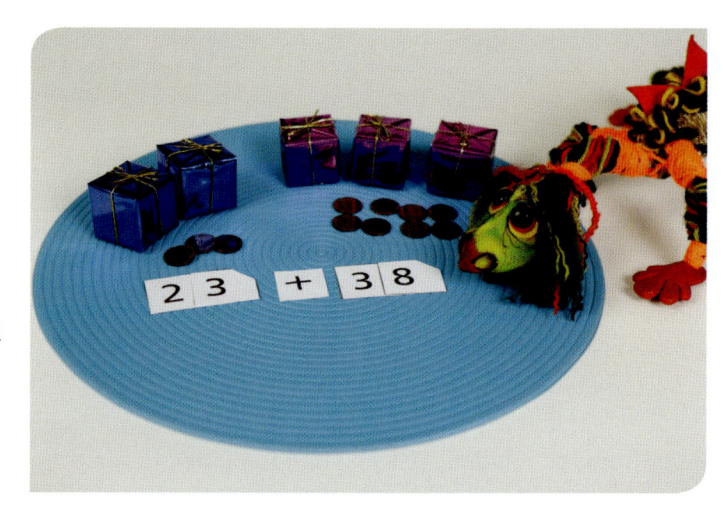

Counting tens and more than ten ones

Many children find it easier to count a quantity where there are nine or fewer single items along with some tens, than if there are tens and more than ten ones.

For example, counting bags of ten buttons and some ones, the child has two things to concentrate on: firstly, switching from counting in tens to counting in ones: "10, 20, 30, 40, **41**, 42, 43, 44, 45, 46, 47, 48 ..." then also crossing a 'decade number' when they count: "49, **50**, 51, 52."

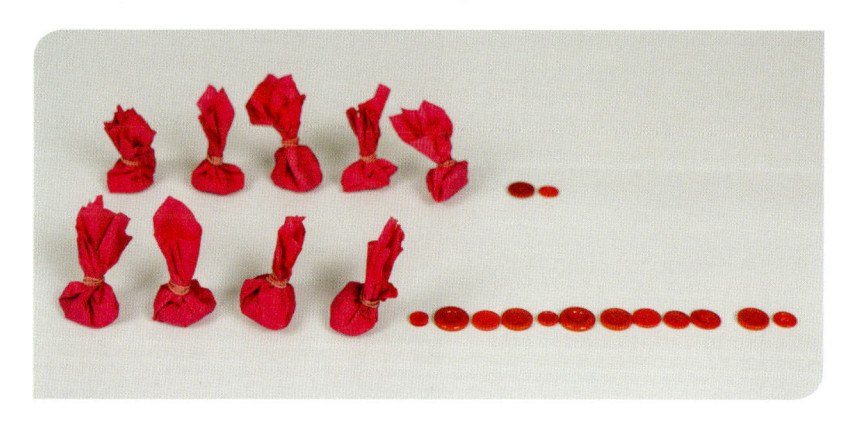

Research link:

Denvir and Brown (1986), in their seminal study of children's work in arithmetic, noted that counting amounts in tens and more than ten ones was an important assessment item and was also an important thing to practise.

Giving children practice in counting mixtures of grouped and ungrouped items will build their confidence when combining amounts. Sometimes, they will count groups of tens and more than ten ones; sometimes they can put extra items together to make another ten; and sometimes they will want to separate a ten into individual items.

More tens and ones

Children can make their own bags of ten small items to use with place value cards, to generate problems to solve with a partner. Initially, ask them to use the cards for 1 to 9 and 10, 20, 30 and 40, and place them face down on the table. Each child picks a ones card and a tens card and makes that number with their bags and single items – then they add the two lots together and write or draw what they have done.

As a development of the activity, children can make three amounts each turn and find their total. They can also extend the range of numbers by using the place value cards for 50 to 90 as well.

Another linked activity is to choose place value cards to make three numbers, and then put them in order from smallest to largest or vice versa.

Children can also choose two numbers and find the difference between them. Sometimes they will want to open one of their bags or boxes to do this.

5 Exploring 25 to 200

COUNTING KEYS

The links between counting in fives and in tens are important ones to make. Since ten is two 5s, we can combine them and count in tens.

Up and down in fives

Find a space where children can sit in a circle. Count up to 100 in fives with successive children holding up a hand for each extra number – by the time you get to 50, ten children will be showing five fingers each! What is the biggest number you can make like this with your circle of children? Ask children to tell you what they think. Count down again putting hands down as you go.

Triangles of tens

We have already explored the triangle you can make with 10 items by using 1 + 2 + 3 + 4. With the keys grouped in tens we have a similar pattern: 10 + 20 + 30 + 40 = 100 (another 'mega fact'!) Children can extend the triangle by adding another row.
Ask: "How many keys would Dragon need to do this?"

Research link:

Fosnot and Dolk (2001) describe a class project which developed from children planting a garden to completing orders for a fictitious seed company. The children grouped five seeds on a card, then put two cards in an envelope to make 10. The teacher was able to see whether and how individual children were using ones, fives or tens to count and record.

COUNTING ON FROM ONE HUNDRED

As we pointed out on page 86, counting on from one hundred can be tricky. Children often miscount saying "98, 99, 100, 110, 120..." or even "98, 99, 100, 200..." There are several ways of helping with this.

- Use two 100 bead strings. Make sure children know there are 100 beads on the first string and count on, on the second string, one bead at a time.

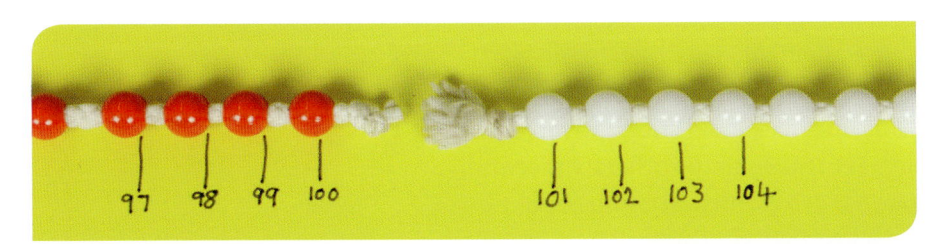

- Use a calculator and say to the children that Dragon had 100 keys and then found one more. Ask children how to work out how many there were altogether on the calculator, by keying in 100 + 1. Imagine Dragon kept finding more keys; ask children to add one again and again until they get to 110.

- Use bags or boxes holding 10s to make 100 and add extra items one at a time counting as you go until you get to 115. Then take away one item at a time, counting aloud together until you get down to 100. Split up one of the tens and keep taking away ones, still counting out loud until you get down to 90. Children can repeat this activity with a partner.

- Children should work with a partner. One child makes a number between 100 and 110 with place value cards. Their partner must match this using 10s and 1s.

Add an extra line or two to your 100 square.

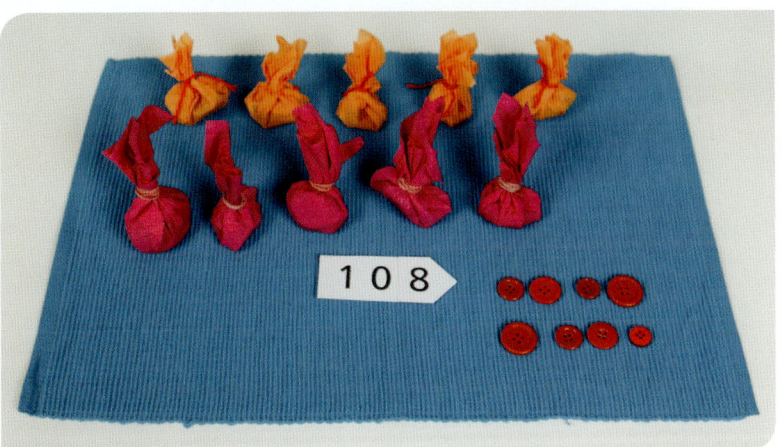

Chapter Five: Exploring 25 to 200

5 Exploring 25 to 200

MAKING TENS AND ONES

Counting large numbers of individual items takes time and leaves us open to losing concentration and making mistakes. As we have shown earlier in this chapter, organizing counting by using groups of ten (and then hundreds, too) alongside ones, helps children to calculate. Children can see that putting things into temporary lines, piles or bundles of 10 is helpful. Making their own equipment with more permanent bundles and groups saves even more time when children are exploring methods of calculation.

For many children, making their equipment is also key to them understanding how to use ready-made hundreds, tens and ones materials effectively: they will be able to see the structure more clearly and know how each element relates to the others. Otherwise, children can seem to know how to reach an answer using bought equipment, but actually they are just following a procedure without really knowing what is going on.

Bags and bundles

Here are some suggestions of items children can collect and count into tens. They can use elastic bands, pipe cleaners or small plastic bags to keep tens together, as appropriate. Children can still see all ten items in these bags or bundles, and can take a ten apart to use the ones in a subtraction or division calculation if needed.

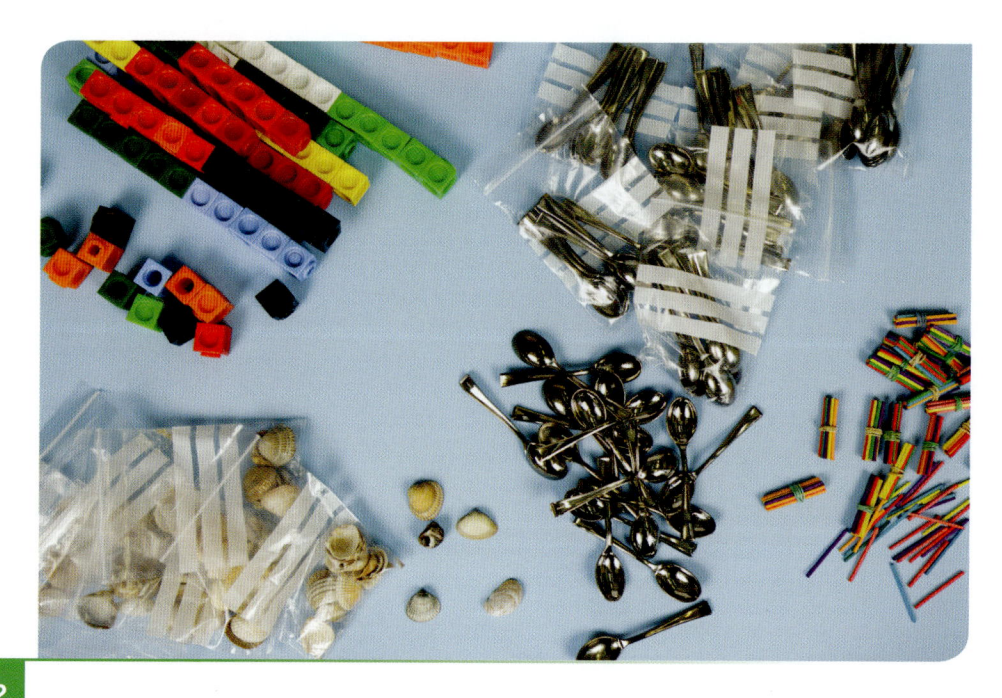

STRINGS, CARDS AND CUT OUTS

A further development is to make tens and ones where you can see and count the ten, but cannot take the tens apart again. That does mean you don't have to check there are still ten!

Here are some suggestions. Make sure there are enough ones in each set of items, so that children can exchange a fixed ten for ten single ones if they want to when calculating.

Hundreds

Once children have made tens and they are confident in counting in tens up to about 120, they can make themselves a 'hundred' to speed up their counting for bigger numbers. Here are some examples. As before, make sure there are enough of the tens and ones in each set, so that children can continue to use tens when they wish.

Research link:

Moscardini (2009) identified teachers either using manipulatives as 'tools' to help children make sense of problems or as 'crutches' to enable them to complete a procedure (often poorly understood). Making and breaking their own 100s, 10s and 1s will help to support children in understanding the structure of ready-made versions.

5 Exploring 25 to 200

HUNDREDS, TENS AND ONES

Once children have had experience of making and using their own tens and ones equipment, they will be better able to see how to use bought equipment in a purposeful and thoughtful way. Although hundreds, tens and ones equipment is often provided in a large storage box, it is more accessible if you keep it in smaller boxes suitable for use by a pair or small group of children.

Make sure children can see that ten 1s are equivalent to a ten; ten 10s to one hundred; and one hundred 1s to 100, too.

Make a number four ways

Children will be more confident with using hundreds, tens and ones equipment when they have had time to explore many different ways of making numbers. Working with a partner, they can try making numbers in several different ways. Here is an example.

Milly and Bhavisha chose a number from cards numbered 40 to 100. They talked about different ways they could make 87 from tens and ones.

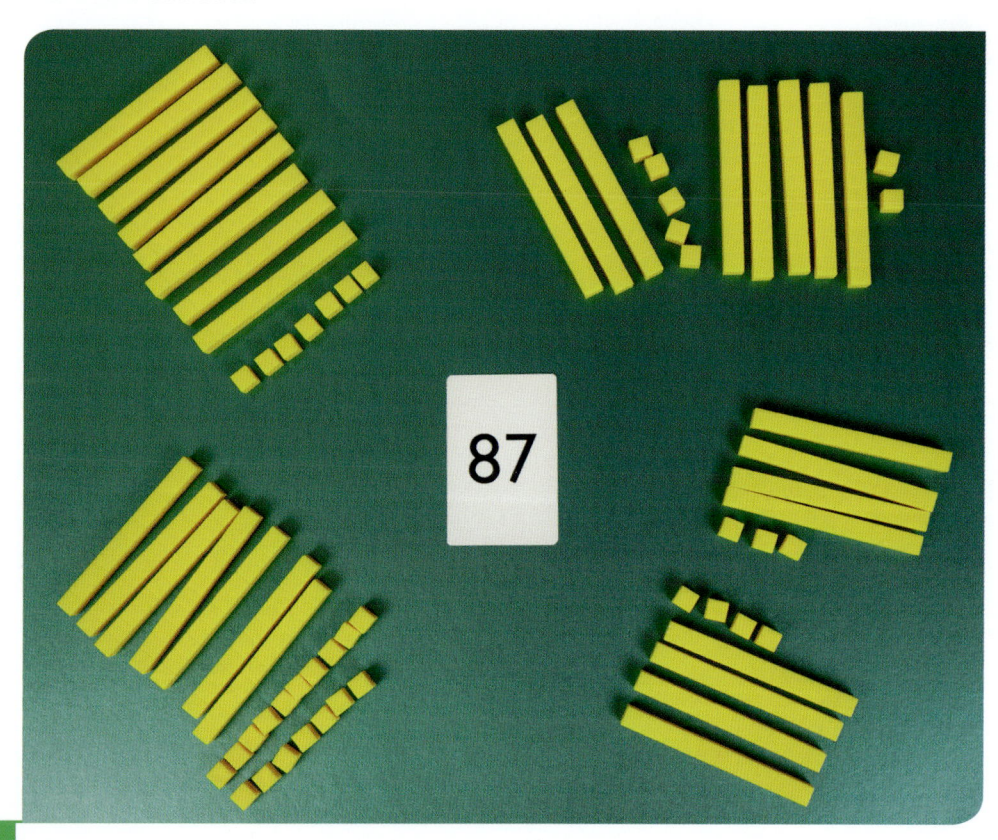

Milly and Bhavisha drew what they had done; they realized quite quickly that they could record their work in an increasingly symbolic fashion. For example, drawing squares, sticks and dots is a simple way of recording work with 100s, 10s and 1s.

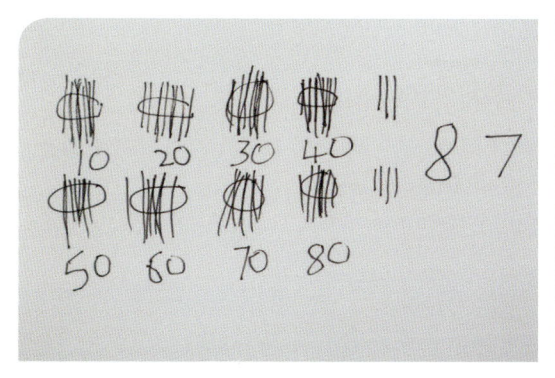

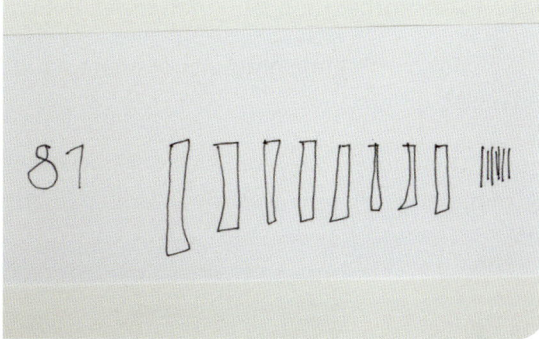

Tens and ones in a line

Children can use 10s and 1s equipment with a matching number line to consolidate their understanding of many principles of addition and subtraction. They can experiment to confirm that you can add in any order, for example 24 add 18 makes 42, whatever order you add in.

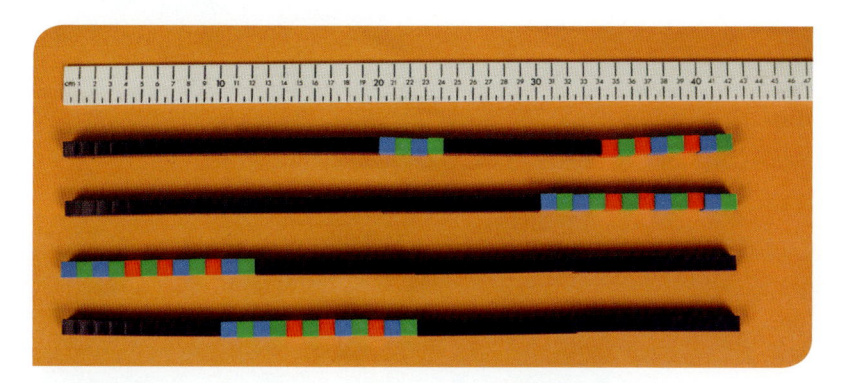

They can also think about multiplying numbers bigger than 10; for example 3 × 12 can also be done as (3 × 10) then adding (3 × 2).

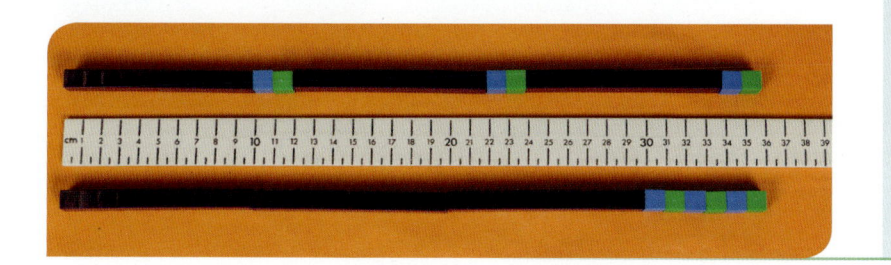

Research link:

Fuson, Smith and Lo Cicero (1997) devised and analyzed a programme of work for children in the USA, using hundreds, tens and ones equipment alongside drawings of numbers as squares, lines and dots. They found that children could use drawings to explore multiple solutions to the calculations they set. They also concluded that work on addition and subtraction with two-digit numbers helped children understand the concept of place value.

Chapter Five: Exploring 25 to 200

95

5 Exploring 25 to 200

MAKING MONEY

Using money in denominations of 1s, 10s and 100s provides another context for calculation. It is more abstract than the tens and ones we have used so far, as each coin or note is a token, rather than being ten times the size of the smaller one.

Children enjoy working with large amounts of money and can design their own £10 and £100 notes.

As children make their notes, they can work out how much money they have got. Discuss ways of making different amounts from a pile of twenty £10 notes:

> How many £1 coins would you need to make £40? £80? £140? £170? £200? Why do you think we use £10 notes?

> We've got twelve £10 notes - how much is that?
> What about twenty £10 notes?

> How many £10 notes do you need to make £40? £80? £140? £170? £200?
> How do you know? What do you notice?

How much?

Children can work with a partner using any of their coins and notes, asking questions like these:

> How much money have I given you?

> Please give me £157!

> We need £240 for a holiday.

> We've got £170. How much more do we need?

96

PACKS AND BOXES

In shops of all kinds, things are packed in boxes and this can offer a meaningful context for exploring multiplication and division. Eggs often come in boxes of six, yoghurts in fours, pencils in fives or 10s and so on. Children can use manipulatives to model one pack of items and help them think about the problem.

Here are some problems they could try:

> There are five pencils in a pack. How many would I have if I had 2 packs, 5 packs, 10 packs, 12 packs? Show me how you worked these out.

> I need 32 pencils for the class. How many packs do I need to buy?

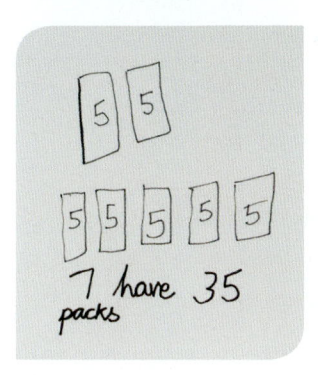

I have 7 packs 35

> There are four yoghurts in a pack. How many would I have if I had 2 packs, 5 packs, 10 packs, 12 packs, 20 packs, 50 packs? Show me how you worked these out.

> We need 129 yoghurts for school dinner. How many packs will we need to order? Show me how you worked this out.

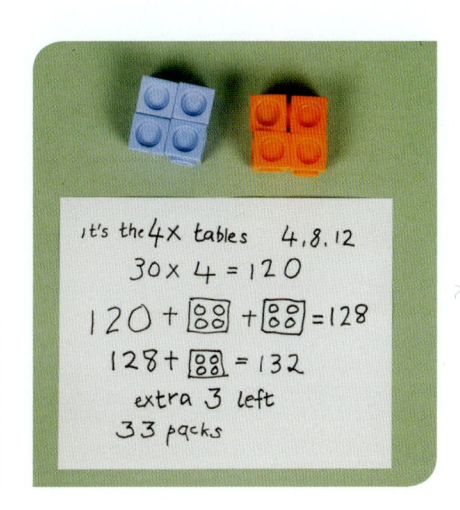

It's the 4x tables 4, 8, 12
30 x 4 = 120
120 + [88] + [88] = 128
128 + [88] = 132
extra 3 left
33 packs

Chapter Five: Exploring 25 to 200

97

5 Exploring 25 to 200

MAKING TIMES TABLES

Once we start considering numbers over 50, the relationships between factors and multiples become more interesting. It is useful to consider multiplication as scaling as well as repeated addition. This can be explored powerfully by building up multiples of a given number using coloured rods.

Seven times as much

The coloured rods on the left show the table of 7s built up by adding 7 each time. The model on the right shows what happens when you take seven 1s, then seven 2s, seven 3s and seven 4s, and shows 'seven times as much'. Both approaches generate the multiples of seven: 7, 14, 21, 28 and so on.

Children can continue this pattern up to 10 × 7. It is interesting for them to discuss why the two different models produce the same number patterns.

They can then do the same with other numbers such as 6, 8, 9, 11 and 12.

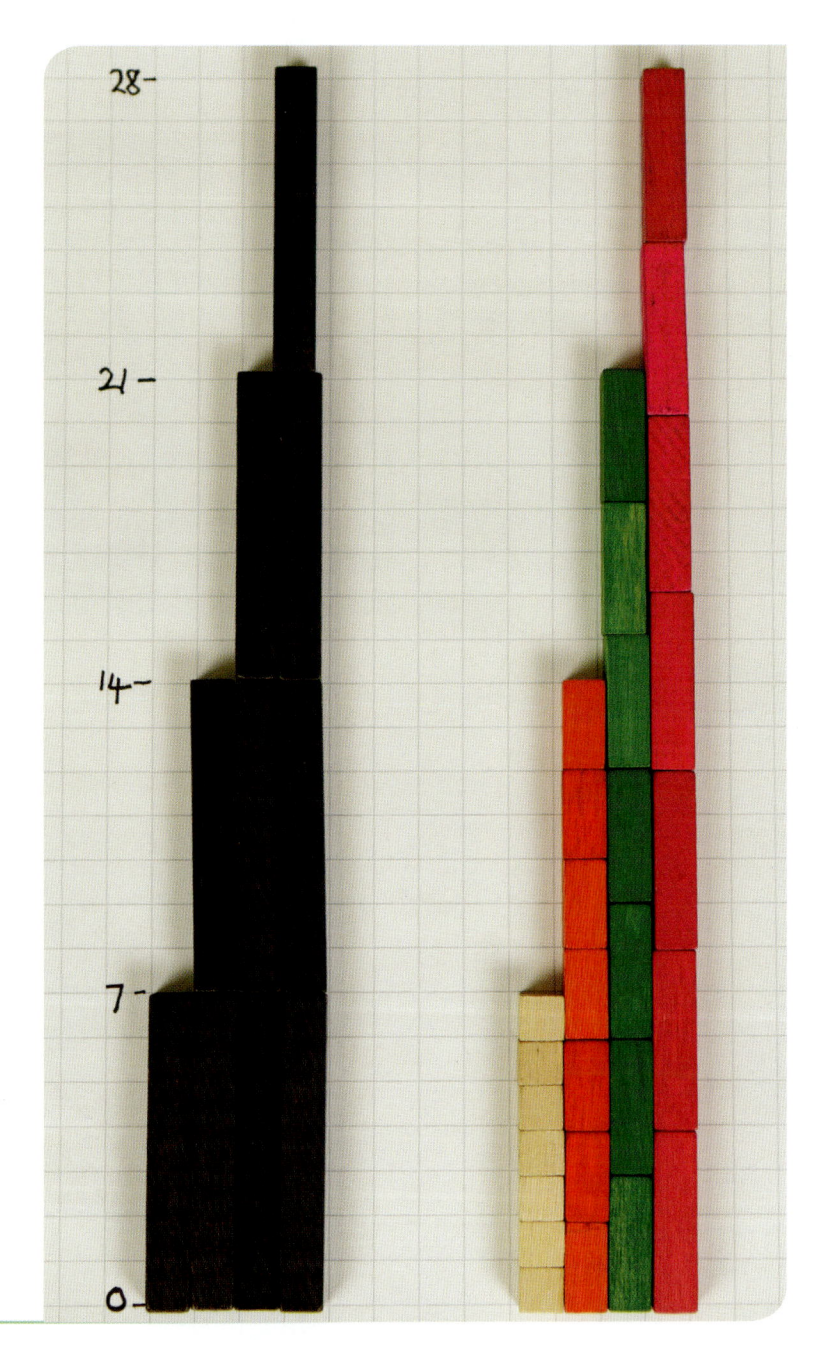

Arrays and times tables

Making arrays for tables by adding successive rows provides a different model to think about. A physical array can also help children learn a few key tables facts, and think about how to derive others from them.

KEY FACTS:

0 × 6 = 0
1 × 6 = 6

5 × 6 = 30 (half of 10 × 6)

10 × 6 = 60

WHAT ELSE CAN YOU WORK OUT?

4 × 6 = 24 (6 less than 30)

6 × 6 = 36 (6 more than 30)

8 × 6 = 48 (double 4 × 6)

9 × 6 = 54 (6 less than 60)

The array can also help children think about the related division facts: for example ask, "How many sixes make 42?" and "Can you make 44 from 6s?"

Changing an array

Choosing one particular array and then thinking about how you can change it can be quite a challenging activity. Here is one example:

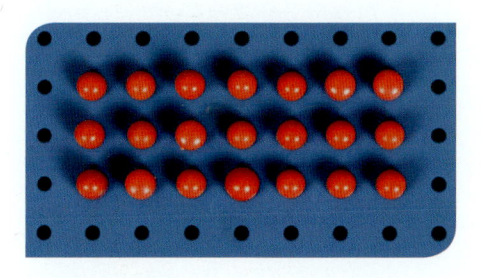

This is 7 × 3?

What is 8 × 3?

Do I add a 7 or a 3?

What is 7 × 4?

Children can work in pairs setting similar questions for each other based on their own arrays.

Chapter Five: Exploring 25 to 200

5 Exploring 25 to 200

TEN TIMES AS MUCH

Multiplying by 10 is a complex concept to explain: doing this practically helps children to see what 'ten times as much' means. You can show this to children with a small number and then let them try the process for themselves. They can then extend the idea to multiplying numbers in the teens by ten.

What happens when you multiply 3 by 10?

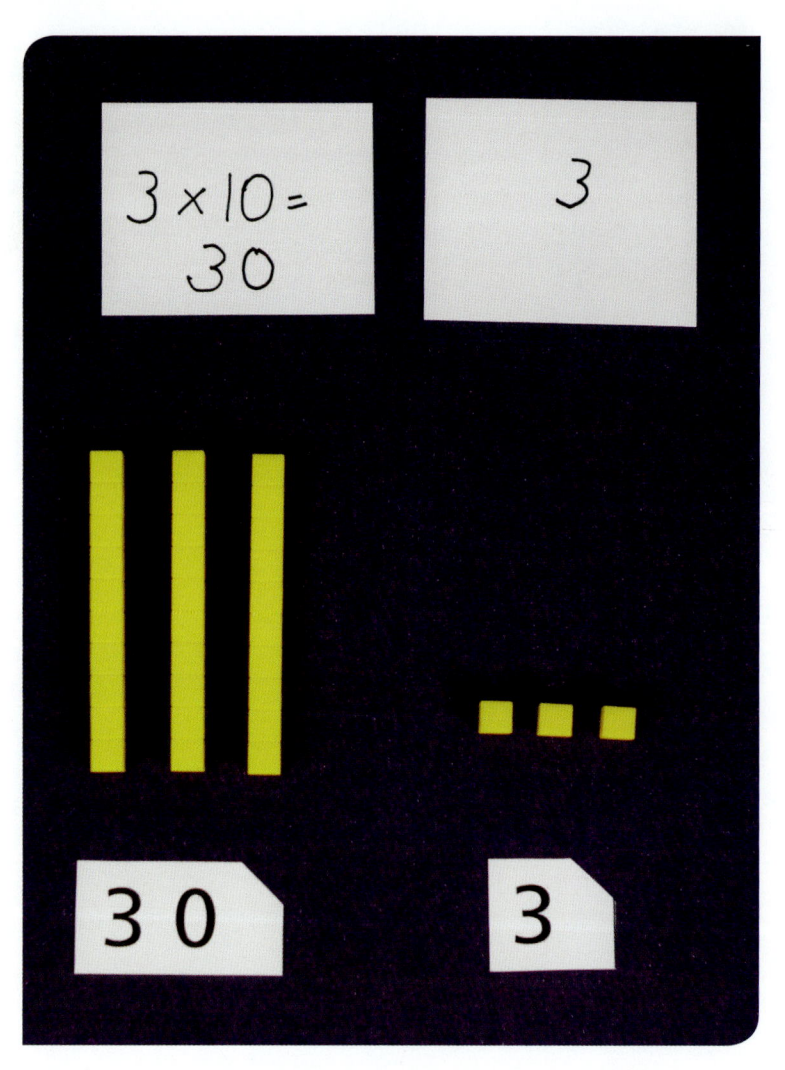

Children can work with a partner to try this for themselves. Ask them to make 4 and 10 lots of 4, or 5 and 10 lots of 5. They should draw and write about what they have found.

> **Research link:**
>
> Thompson (2000) discusses the different ways that children will think about numbers like 37 in terms of place value and introduces the ideas of *quantity value (30 and 7)* and *column value (3 tens and 7 ones)*.
>
> Ruthven (1998) reported on a major project using calculators to explore number, which found that calculators could support children's understanding in arithmetic and their development of mental methods.

Practise swaps

It is useful to check that children understand that ten 1s is the same as one 10 and that ten 10s is the same as one 100.

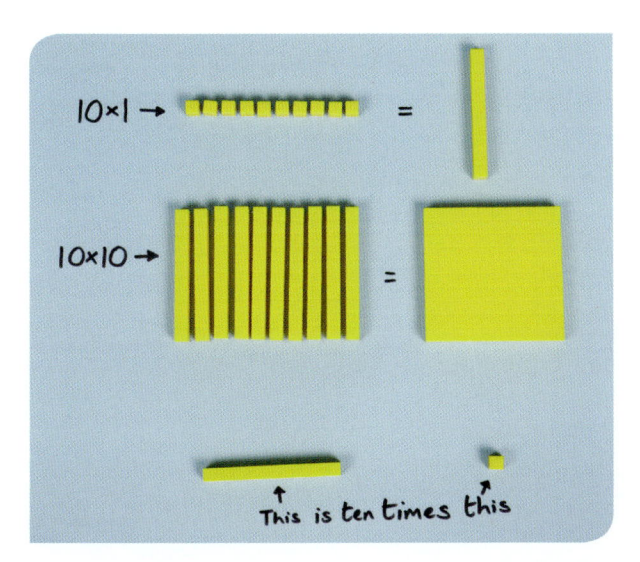

This is ten times this

Ten times teens

Children can choose a number between 10 and 20. The first child makes that number with 10s and 1s and with place value cards. They ask their partner to make ten times as much with 1s, 10s and a 100 and to match it with place value cards. They can also see what happens when they multiply by ten on a calculator.

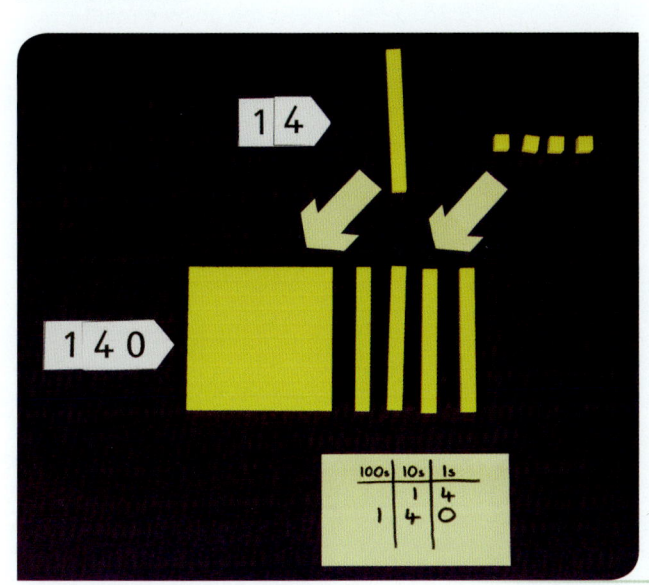

Please give me 10 times as much.

Chapter Five: Exploring 25 to 200

5 Exploring 25 to 200

MULTIPLYING TEENS

Children often find it helpful to be able to explore an idea in several different ways, using a mixture of work with manipulatives, talking and drawing.

Many of the mental methods that adults use, whether they are adding, subtracting, multiplying or dividing, rely on *rounding*. This can be to get a rough answer when we do not need an accurate one – for example, you may add like this when you are totting up a shopping basket while you are going round the supermarket. For adults and children, rounding is very useful as a way of checking the reasonableness of a calculation.

Thinking about rough answers

Peter's class were thinking about how to get an idea of how big their answer should be, when they multiplied a teens number by any number from 3 to 9.

The first suggestion Peter made was that they could think about what they knew already.

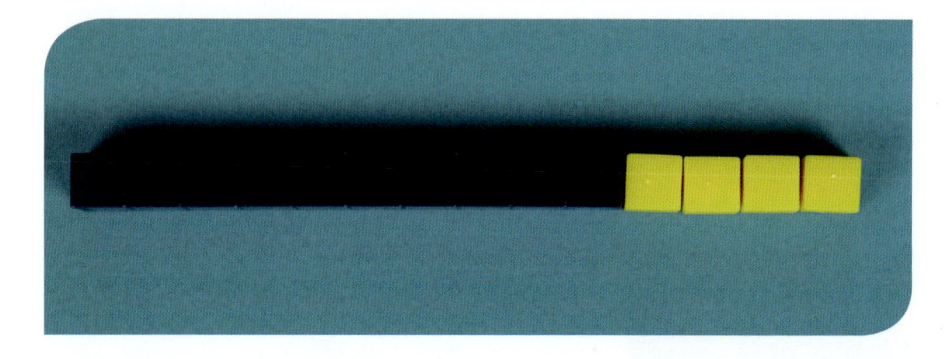

> Suppose you want to make 3 × 14. What do you know already?

> Three lots of ten is 30. So the answer must be more than 30!

Children also thought about numbers that would be bigger than the answer they were calculating.

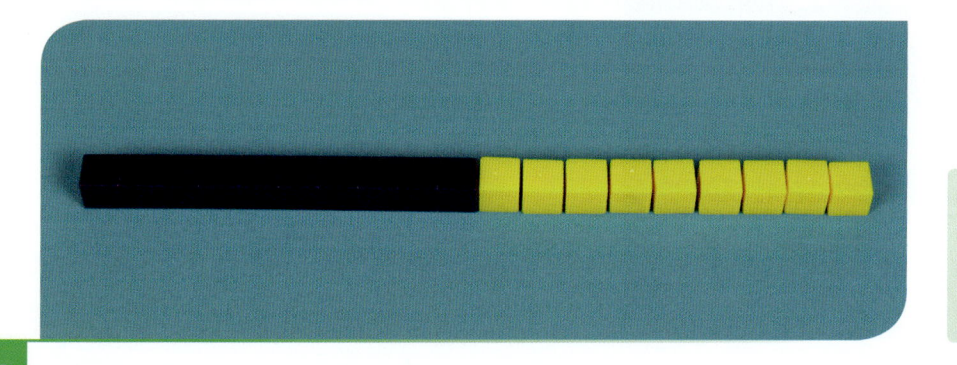

> Suppose you want to make 3 × 19. 19 is nearly 20 …

> Three lots of twenty is 60. 3 × 20 is more than we need. So the answer for 3 × 19 must be less than 60!

Thinking about multiplying

Holly and Nino built on their earlier work with arrays and times tables to think about multiplying 18 by 4. They worked together, aiming to show other children as many ways as they could of thinking about this calculation. Here are some of their ideas.

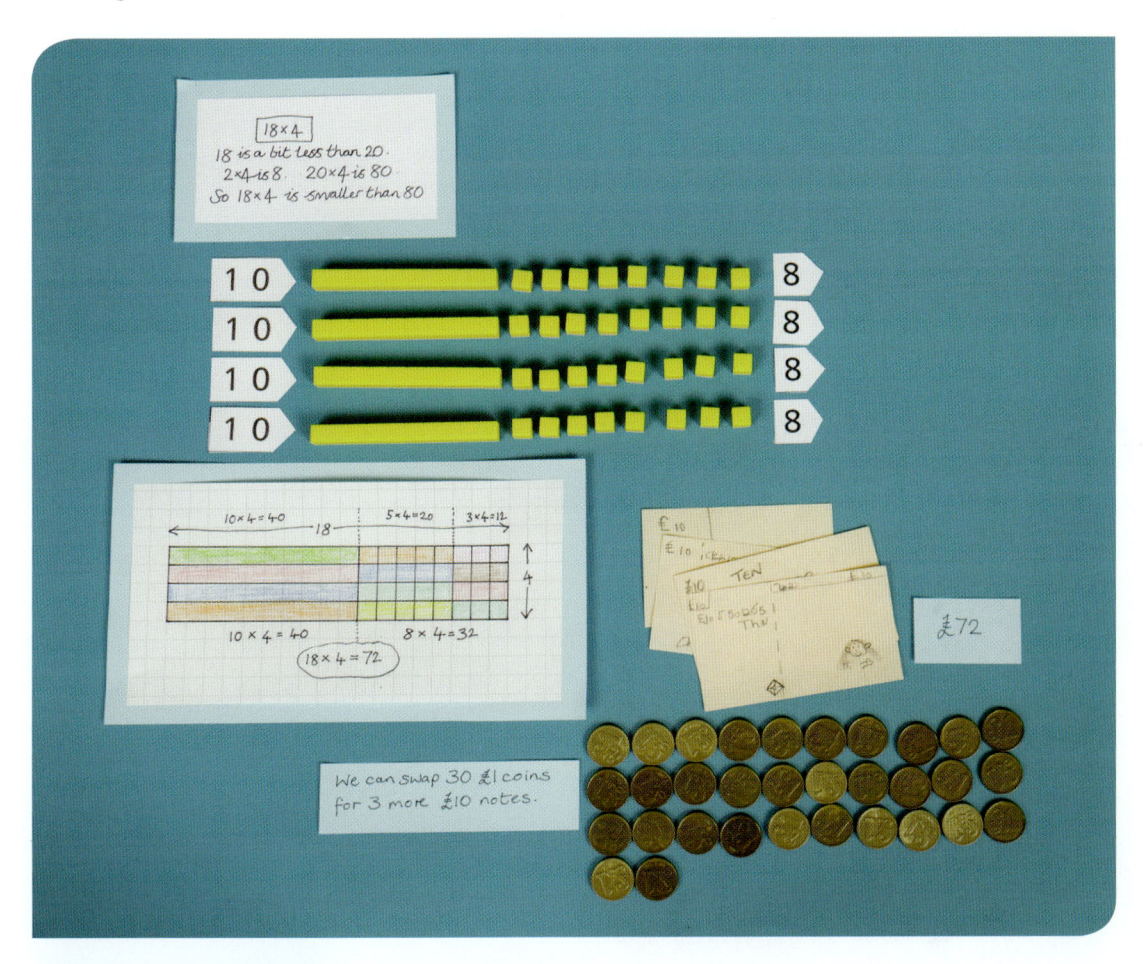

18 × 4
18 is a bit less than 20.
2 × 4 is 8. 20 × 4 is 80.
So 18 × 4 is smaller than 80.

10 | 8
10 | 8
10 | 8
10 | 8

10 × 4 = 40 — 18 — 5 × 4 = 20 | 3 × 4 = 12
10 × 4 = 40 | 8 × 4 = 32
18 × 4 = 72

£72

We can swap 30 £1 coins for 3 more £10 notes.

1 1 8
1 1 8
1 1 8
1 1 8

Other children in the class worked in pairs on calculations they chose for themselves, using any teens number multiplied by a single digit number. Some started to think about more difficult calculations, by adding an extra ten to their teen number. For example, what is 28 × 4? Some tried adding one hundred: what is 118 × 4?

Chapter Five: Exploring 25 to 200

103

5 Exploring 25 to 200

EXPLORING DIVISION

Division is an aspect of arithmetic that many people find difficult – often because they have been moved on too quickly to using standard pencil and paper methods before they really understood the principles behind them. There are two key ideas to think about: *grouping* and *sharing*. Each represents a different context for division.

Division and multiplication can be tackled together, and the idea of *grouping* has been explored earlier in this book, including when looking at arrays. For example, children can think about 4 lots of 3, multiplying to make 12; they can also divide: how many groups of 3 can you make from 12?

Here, we will concentrate on ideas of *sharing*, and helping children to explore sharing numbers in a systematic way. Children can choose a number and then divide in turn by 2, then 3, then 4 and so on, to see what happens. You can begin by modelling the process with an example to raise some of the issues they will need to discuss with their partner.

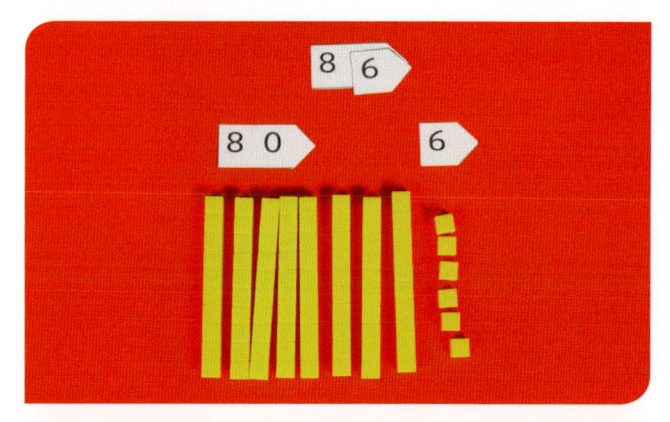

> I've chosen the number 86 to explore. First, I'll think about how the number is made.

> Imagine I am going to share 86 things equally between 2 people. It could be 86 marbles, 86 badges, 86 pencils, 86 oranges, £86 … my tens and ones can stand for any items I want to share.

> It's easy to share 86 between two. 86 ÷ 2 = 43. None left over!

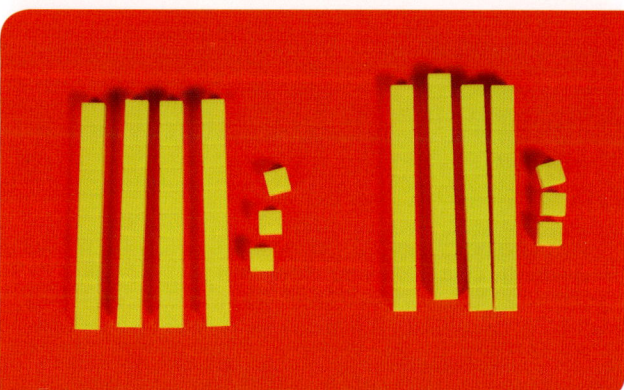

Now imagine I want to share 86 things equally between three people. 20 each to start with, leaving 26 more to share between three.

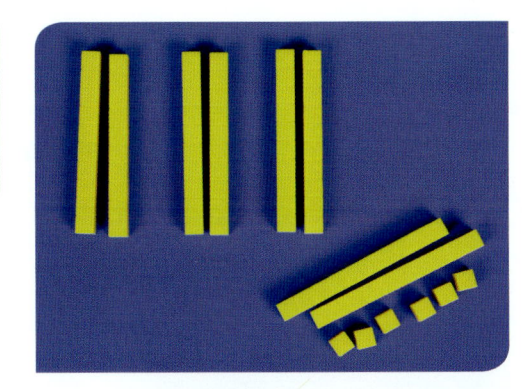

I can think of that 26 as ones, then give the three people one each, then one more each, and so on. I need 3 each time I give one to each person. How many 3s have I got?

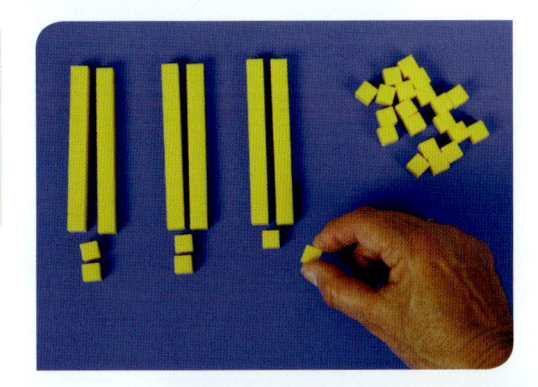

I can make eight 3s – that's 24. So I can give them 8 each, and I'll have 2 left over. So 86 divided by 3 is 28, remainder 2.

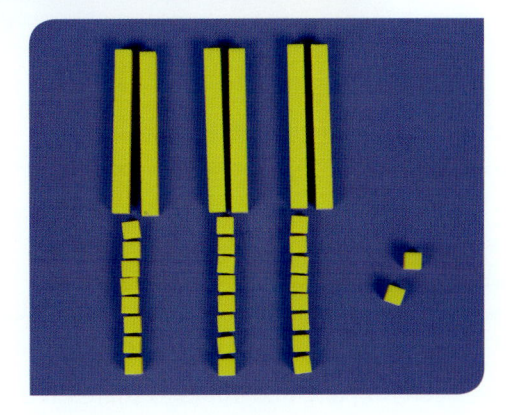

The context of a problem will help children to decide what happens to the remainder. For example, oranges can be cut up, so sharing oranges may involve fractions. Badges cannot be cut up so sharing them may leave whole number remainders.

When children divide a number by 2 then 3, then 4 and so on, they should see that the amount each person gets becomes smaller.

In the example above, children can begin to see the connections between sharing and grouping. Using manipulatives encourages children to explore and discuss the ways in which different ideas in mathematics fit together.

Chapter Five: Exploring 25 to 200

105

Chapter Six: Looking Forward

Looking at the use of manipulatives has confirmed some of our ideas, challenged others and made us dig deeper into children's understanding.

Manipulatives are things to think with in a way that is different from work with pencil and paper. They are part of a repertoire of approaches for exploring numbers and how they work.

Tony, a teacher in year 4 said:

> I was thinking about how I explain things in everyday life. Haven't you ever used salt and pepper pots and a ketchup bottle to explain how you get from A to B? And yet it has surprised me to see how much easier children find it to explain their thinking, when they have things to move about! It really does make their thinking more transparent.

Even the simplest ideas in mathematics may be more complex than we first appreciate so we need to give children time to experiment and make their own decisions. We must also balance this with times when we suggest ways of working. Modern technologies can support both approaches, by using visualizers or webcams. Children and teachers can demonstrate what they have been thinking and doing to share their mathematical reasoning:

> A resource which facilitates demonstration and interaction mediates discussion in powerful ways. It offers the possibility for teachers to support their talk with appropriate actions and, in turn, to watch and listen to pupils interacting with the same resource, revealing their inherent understanding of important concepts as well as any potential misconceptions. (Delaney 2010: 82)

Used effectively, activity with equipment can support children in analyzing and solving problems, spotting patterns and relationships and explaining to others what they have learnt. A growing body of neuroscientific research endorses this view:

> … Physical interaction with the world is a critical part of knowledge construction … sensory-motor representations … are augmented by knowledge gained through action, language, pretend play and teaching.
> (Goswami & Bryant 2007:7)

We have known for a while that effective teachers of mathematics are:

- making connections within mathematics, both between different aspects of mathematics… and between different representations of mathematics – symbols, words, diagrams and objects;
- making connections with children's methods – valuing these and being interested in children's thinking but also sharing other methods. (Askew 2012: 35).

Being 'good at mathematics' has many aspects. One way that mathematical proficiency has been described is as a rope with five strands (Kilpatrick, Swafford and Findell 2001). Two of these strands focus on solving problems: *strategic competence* and *adaptive reasoning*. Our emphasis on children taking the initiative and making decisions supports both of these. These strands, together with *conceptual understanding, procedural fluency* and *productive disposition*, can all be developed by the use of manipulatives.

Sometimes our beliefs about what we need to teach are challenged by new research. Procedural fluency is frequently thought of as dependent on having speedy recall of number facts. However, a study led by Cowan (2011) found that high achieving children were more likely to use their understanding of the structure of the number system to derive number facts as they needed them rather than knowing lots by heart. Manipulatives can help children to understand that structure.

Chapter Six: Looking Forward

107

6 Looking Forward

ENJOYING WORKING WITH NUMBERS

Learning should be enjoyable and purposeful but not so pressured that children are rushed ahead before they have had a chance to understand what is happening. As Razia said:

> We spent a whole lesson on the number 18 last week and the children got so much out of it. It convinced me how important it is to allow children time to explore.

Using equipment can be especially helpful to children who are developing their language skills. Ishaaq was new to English and his teacher said:

> We were looking at the number staircase from 1 to 20. I could see that Ishaaq had spotted the repeating pattern because he pointed to the towers for 11, 12, and 13 saying, "One, two, three," and then gestured towards the towers for 1, 2 and 3. Then Tehmina said, "Eleven, twelve, thirteen. It's the same pattern as one, two, three." Ishaaq said, "Yes, yes," and repeated, "Eleven, twelve, thirteen."

Even the very youngest children can enjoy the important learning sequence that is sometimes called 'Do, Talk, Record'. Leo and Robin were putting people in the boats and telling each other how many were going sailing. They argued for some time about what number they should put next to each boat and then on their drawing but eventually agreed the total was six.

We are aiming to continue reading, experimenting and writing about how children can gain a thorough understanding of the number system in an active, purposeful and interesting way. We hope our work so far has encouraged you to try things out and to think about ideas you want to explore. There is plenty more to do!

REFERENCES

Askew, M. (2012) *Transforming Primary Mathematics.* Abingdon: Routledge.

Barmby, P., Harries, T. & Higgins, S. (2010) 'Teaching for Understanding/ Understanding for Teaching.' Chapter 3 in Thompson, I. (Ed.) *Issues in Teaching Numeracy in Primary Schools,* 2nd Edition. Maidenhead: Open University Press/McGraw-Hill Education. 45–57.

Beishuizen, M. (2010) 'The Empty Number Line' Chapter 13 in Thompson, I. (Ed.) *Issues in Teaching Numeracy in Primary Schools,* 2nd Edition. Maidenhead: Open University Press/McGraw-Hill Education. 174–187.

Boaler, J. (2009) *The Elephant in the Classroom: Helping Children Learn and Love Maths.* London: Souvenir Press.

Bobis, J., Mulligan, J. & Lowrie, T. (2013) *Mathematics for Children: Challenging Children to Think Mathematically,* 4th Edition. New South Wales: Pearson.

Bruner, J. (1966) *Toward a Theory of Instruction.* Cambridge, Massachusetts: Harvard University Press.

Buys, K. (2001) 'Pre-School Years – Emergent Numeracy', in M. Van Den Heuvel-Panhuizen (Ed.) *Children Learn Mathematics: A Learning-Teaching Trajectory with Intermediate Targets for Calculation with Whole Numbers in Primary School,* Utrecht: Freudenthal Institute. 25–30.

Cobb, P. (1995) 'Cultural Tools and Mathematical Learning: A Case Study.' *Journal for Research in Mathematics Education,* 26 (4), 362–385.

Cowan, R., Donlan, C., Shepherd, D., Cole-Fletcher, R., Saxton, M. & Hurry, J. (2011) 'Basic Calculation Proficiency and Mathematics Achievement in Elementary School Children'. *Journal of Educational Psychology,* 103 (4), 786–803.

Delaney, K. (2010) 'Making Connections: Teachers and Children Using Resources Effectively.' in I. Thompson (Ed.) *Issues in Teaching Numeracy in Primary Schools,* 2nd Edition. Maidenhead: Open University Press/McGraw-Hill Education. 72–83.

Denvir, B. & Brown, M. (1986) 'Understanding of Number Concepts in Low Attaining 7–9 Year Olds: Part 1. Development of Descriptive Framework and Diagnostic Instrument.' *Educational Studies in Mathematics,* 17 (1), 15–36.

Fosnot, C. T. & Dolk, M. (2001) *Young Mathematicians at Work: Constructing Number Sense, Addition, and Subtraction.* Portsmouth, New Hampshire: Heinemann.

Fuson, K. C. (1998) *Children's Counting and Concepts of Number.* New York: Springer-Verlag.

Fuson, K. C., Smith, S. T. & Lo Cicero, A. M. (1997) 'Supporting Latino First Graders' Ten-Structured Thinking in Urban Classrooms.' *Journal for Research in Mathematics Education,* 28 (6), 738–766.

Gelman, R. & Gallistel, C. R. (1978) *The Child's Understanding of Number.* Cambridge, Mass.: Harvard University Press.

Goswami, U. & Bryant, P. (2007) *Children's Cognitive Development and Learning.* (Primary Review Research Survey 2/1a). Cambridge: University of Cambridge Faculty of Education.

Goutard, M. (1964) *Mathematics and Children.* Reading: Educational Explorers Ltd.

Gray, E. & Tall, D. (1994) 'Duality, Ambiguity, and Flexibility: A 'Proceptual' View of Simple Arithmetic.' *Journal for Research in Mathematics Education*, 25 (2), 116–140.

Hughes, M. (1986) *Children and Number: Difficulties in Learning Mathematics.* Oxford: Blackwell.

Kilpatrick, J., Swafford, J. & Findell, B. (Eds) (2001) *Adding It Up: Helping Children Learn Mathematics.* Washington: National Academy Press.

Mason, J., Burton, L. & Stacey, K. (2010) *Thinking Mathematically,* 2nd Edition. Harlow: Pearson.

Moscardini, L. (2009) 'Tools or Crutches? Apparatus as a Sense-Making Aid in Mathematics Teaching with Children with Moderate Learning Difficulties'. *Support for Learning,* 24 (1), 35–41. Oxford: Nasen.

Mulligan, J. & Mitchelmore, M. (2009). 'Awareness of Pattern and Structure in Early Mathematical Development'. *Mathematics Education Research Journal*, 21 (2), 33–49.

Munn, P. (2008) 'Children's Beliefs About Counting', Chapter 2 in I. Thompson Ed.) *Issues in Teaching Numeracy in Primary Schools,* 2nd Edition. Maidenhead: Open University Press/McGraw-Hill Education. 19–33.

Nunes, T. & Bryant. P, (2009) *Key Understandings in Mathematics Learning. Paper 2: Understanding Whole Numbers.* London: Nuffield Foundation.

Ruthven, K. (1998) 'The Use of Mental, Written And Calculator Strategies of Numerical Computation by Upper Primary Pupils within a 'Calculator-Aware' Number Curriculum'. *British Educational Research Journal,* 24 (1), 21–42.

Sarama, J. & Clements, D. H. (2009) *Early Childhood Mathematics Education Research: Learning Trajectories for Young Children.* London: Routledge.

Thompson, I. (2000) 'Teaching Place Value in the UK: Time for a Reappraisal?' *Educational Review*, 52 (3), 291–298.

Wynn, K. (1990) 'Children's Understanding of Counting.' *Cognition*. 36 (2), 155–93.

Wright, R. J., Stanger, G., Stafford, A. K. & Martland, J. (2014) *Teaching Number in the Classroom with 4–8 Year Olds,* 2nd Edition. London: Sage.

Quick reference

Topic	Page
animation	20–25, 38–43, 64–69, 82–91
addition	8, 9, 21–25, 28–29, 32–35, 38, 41, 52–53, 66, 74–87, 79, 82–84, 86–89
arrays	55, 57, 60, 66, 70–71, 84–85, 99
base ten apparatus	see hundreds, tens and ones
bead strings	35–36, 41, 48–49, 69, 76–77, 91
calculator	33, 46–47, 56, 67, 79
comparison/comparing	11, 16–17, 28, 31, 34, 44–45,62– 63, 79, 88–89
composition	11, 22–25, 29–30, 34, 35, 42– 43, 48–49, 79, 83–85
counting	11, 13–29, 32, 34, 39, 44–45, 57–58, 60–61, 64–65, 80– 83, 87, 91
counting in groups	39, 57, 59, 60–61, 66–69, 78, 79–81, 84–85, 88–90
coloured rods	12, 49, 51–53, 72–73, 98
cubes, linked/interlocking	8, 10, 13, 35, 41, 46, 49–50, 92–93, 97
difference	56, 89
division	42, 57, 67, 70–71, 78, 84–85, 104–105
doubling and halving	54, 67
estimating	79, 102
factors	61, 70–73
home-made hundreds, tens and ones	63, 74–75, 88–89, 92–93
hundred square	82–83, 91
hundreds, tens and ones	7, 12, 74–75, 84, 88–96, 100–105
manipulatives (definition)	7
mega facts	68, 86, 90
missing number problems	21, 25, 43, 52–53, 69, 81
money	11, 80, 96, 103
multiples	61, 70–73, 78, 98–99
multiplication	55, 57, 70–73, 78, 84–85, 97–103
number bonds or facts	38, 41–43, 52–54, 68–69, 76–78, 82– 87, 98–99
number frames	13, 39
number lines	47, 49, 95
number sense (definition)	11
number tracks	49, 82–83
odd and even	35, 39, 59
one more than/one less than	28, 35, 50
partitioning	42–43, 74–75
pattern spotting	39–41, 54, 68–69, 90–91
place value (definition)	62
place value cards	46, 47, 62, 63, 88–89
subitizing (definition)	30
subtraction	21, 24–25, 32–33, 35, 37–38, 52–53, 56, 57, 74–77, 82–83, 86–89,
ten-frames	54
unitizing (definition)	66
zero/nought/none	21, 78, 79